MAKING

Parish Policy

A Workbook on Sacramental Policies

MAKING

Parish Policy

A Workbook on Sacramental Policies

Ron Lewinski

LITURGY TRAINING PUBLICATIONS

Acknowledgments

Excerpts from *Archdiocese of Chicago Policies and Procedures, Book IV: The Sanctifying Office of the Church* are reprinted by permission of the Office of the Chancellor. The book is a work in progress and only the sections on initiation, Sunday eucharist and other liturgies, penance, marriage, and funerals are reprinted here.

Copies of the full text of *Book IV,* including the sections on faculties and sacramental records, which are not in *Making Parish Policy,* may be obtained by mail or fax from New World Publications, Policy and Procedure Handbook Offer, 1144 West Jackson Blvd., Chicago IL 60607; FAX 312-243-1526.

Editor: Martin F. Connell
Production editor: Deborah Bogaert
Design: Jill Smith
Typesetting: Jim Mellody-Pizzato
Printed by BookCrafters.

ISBN 1-56854-116-3

contents

Introduction

I have been involved in the liturgical apostolate for more than two decades. When one of my friends and colleagues heard I was preparing this work-book on policies and procedures, he was taken aback and responded, "Why in the world are you writing a workbook on policies and procedures?"

His reaction was understandable. "Policies and procedures" sounds like "laws," which sounds restrictive and legalistic. Those two words conjure up thoughts of rubricism. But people's reactions to "policies and procedures" probably say more about our past experiences of church law and rubrics than about our experiences with them today. Perhaps we remember more of what we couldn't do than what we could do, or, more importantly, what the intentions were behind the laws.

In my ten years as director of the Office for Divine Worship of the archdiocese of Chicago, I was struck not by how much pastoral ministers felt burdened by church law but by how uncertain they were as to what the liturgical or sacramental norms of the church might be on any particular issue. This was not because they didn't study the primary liturgical sources but because in many cases, the sources were not clear or were even silent about an issue. Furthermore, I learned that even where the church's norms were clear, the interpretation and application to parish practice could be very difficult to achieve. Pastors often found themselves in quandaries about what to do.

I also would receive many calls when there was a question about what the archdiocesan position might be on an issue. Frankly, in some cases I didn't know the answer. Sometimes I was able to retrieve some documentation from the files, sometimes a call to the chancellor's office resolved the question, and at other times the chancellor or myself and the office staff, or all of us together, had to make a decision as each case presented itself.

What became evident to me was that pastoral ministers did not have guidance and support from clear policies and procedures that they could rely upon to help them make confident and competent decisions at the parish level. I learned to trust that the pastoral ministers who called the worship office valued the liturgy and the celebration of the sacraments. They were conscientious about observing the law, but they were equally concerned about making the appropriate applications of the law while respecting the integrity of the liturgy as it was celebrated in their particular communities.

I came across many parishes that wanted to formulate their own policies and procedures for parish sacramental life but didn't know where to begin or how best to address the issues. Nevertheless, many have been working hard at it and have been successful; I have learned from their experiences. Others have been less than successful, but I have learned with them, too, from those experiences.

In 1989, Cardinal Bernardin announced the formation of a sacramental task force for the archdiocese of Chicago that would review the sacramental life of the archdiocese and propose a set of sacramental policies and procedures. Its tasks were to review current practice, evaluate whatever policies and procedures were already in place and begin drafting sacramental policies and procedures that could serve as a supportive structure for parish ministers faced with establishing policy and practice on the parish level. From the very start the task force understood that the archbishop's mandate was not intended as a "corrective" but as another stage of the ongoing work of liturgical renewal. Underlying the massive project was a genuine pastoral concern for how we could revive Catholic sacramental life and celebrate the rites of the church with meaning, dignity and respect for the integrity of the rites.

The primary concern was for God's people, who are growing in diversity. How could they best be served in a time of fewer resources, including fewer ordained ministers? The policies were drafted with a sensitivity for the church's ministers, who often feel heavily burdened by increasing sacramental demands, and with a desire to provide archdiocesan policies and procedures that could serve as the parameters within which parish communities would formulate parish policies and procedures to best serve their needs.

The process of the task force eventually led to the publication of *Book IV: Sacramental Policies and Procedures for the Archdiocese of Chicago.* As the task force for sacramental practices worked diligently to formulate archdiocesan policies and procedures for sacramental life, there were other task forces updating and formulating policies and procedures on other matters of church life, such as administration and personnel. The work of these other projects is published in Books I, II and III. The content of each book corresponds to each book of the *Code of Canon Law.* Thus *Book IV: Sacramental Policies and Procedures for the Archdiocese of Chicago* corresponds to *The Sanctifying Office of the Church,* Book IV of the *Code of Canon Law.*

The task force took three years to complete its work. The process involved study and research, numerous meetings and several drafts. The most important part of the process was the extensive consultation that reached into every corner of the archdiocese. Although this took a long time, the task force quickly learned the value of pondering the issues from several angles. Our own assumptions about liturgy and sacraments were challenged often. Again and again we had to return to original sources to study the church's intent in each of the rites. As a result, we found ourselves renewed in our own appreciation for the sacramental life of the church.

We began to envision what might happen if parish communities went through a similar process of developing sacramental policies and procedures at the parish level. Our hope and prayer then was not just to produce well-written policies and procedures but through them to foster a renewal in sacramental life. This is one of the primary goals of this workbook: to encourage and facilitate the renewal of sacramental life in parish communities through the process of developing their own policies and procedures.

How to Use This Book

This workbook has several components. Parts of *Sacramental Policies and Procedures of the Archdiocese of Chicago* are provided throughout the book and in the second part of the book to give you a picture of how one diocesan church formulated its concerns. We will draw from these sacramental policies and procedures for our examples, but the sacramental policies and procedures of the archdiocese of Chicago are only a sample of what sacramental policies and procedures might look like. The sample isn't perfect: Since its promulgation, we have already begun to see where we might have been deficient. But it was our understanding that these policies and procedures would go through revisions in the years ahead, which is the reason for the elaborate numbering system that allows adding or revising a policy or procedure without having to reprint the entire document.

The primary purpose of this workbook is to invite you to review the sacramental practices of your parish and to consider what kinds of parish policies and procedures might be helpful for the community and would most fittingly express the community's experience of the presence of God as mediated through the church and in sacramental life. The exercises in this book will give you a sense of how you might go about addressing an issue and developing your own policies and procedures. Hopefully, the exercises will give you a feel for a method and for the kinds of questions you might ask in the process. Remember, it is not just the end product that will be important. A review of the parish's sacramental life can be very fruitful when sufficient time is taken to revisit the liturgical sources and to reflect on pastoral experience.

Formulating sacramental policies and procedures can be an overwhelming task; it is a vast field. But it is not necessary for a parish to attempt a comprehensive work that covers every aspect of sacramental life. When setting out to formulate policies and procedures, begin with the essentials and the issues that recur frequently. Define the parameters of the work. Let the work respond to needs so that it does not become an abstract academic exercise. If a long-range plan is established, the work can be done in several phases over a number of years.

While the focus of this book will be the parish, what is found here can easily be adapted and applied to the diocese as a whole. Diocesan staff will find that the methods and processes suggested here can likewise be used to revisit, review or reformulate diocesan sacramental policies and procedures.

A Word of Gratitude

In producing this workbook I am most grateful to all who served on the archdiocesan sacramental task force. Most of the ideas in this book were at one point or another generated by that task force.

In a special way I wish to thank Robert Tuzik, who patiently devoted himself to researching Chicago's sacramental policies and procedures and to considering the revisions proposed in the process of several consultations; Robert Kealy, Thomas Paprocki, and Michael Place, who brought their expertise in theology and canon law to the task force; Mary Anne O'Ryan, OSB, another task force member, to whom I owe most of the ideas in chapter four; John Huels, OSM, for his canonical and liturgical advice; Gabe Huck, who encouraged this project; and Martin Connell, the editor, who brought this book to its final form. Finally, I want to thank Joseph Cardinal Bernardin, whose vision in establishing the sacramental task force and whose support and interest in the project brought the work to a fruitful end.

Ron Lewinski

Why Policies and Procedures?

It is the ongoing work of liturgical renewal that gives rise to the need for sacramental policies and procedures. But liturgical renewal involves far more than the revision of the liturgical books — it requires a sensitivity to the way in which the rites are celebrated. The style or manner of a celebration can have a tremendous impact on how the rites affect us. How we prepare for the liturgy and how decisions are made about legitimate pastoral options and adaptations have significant pastoral and spiritual implications. And underlying all of this is a spirituality that calls us as church to celebrate the liturgy with full, conscious and active faith. Rubrical observance alone is not sufficient; the underlying belief is that through the liturgy we give fullest expression to what it means to be church. Liturgy then is not something apart from who we are as church. Liturgy shapes the community's identity by establishing an order that over time fashions us into a Catholic people. Liturgical renewal requires a commitment to celebrating the liturgy with style and grace and with converted hearts.

Establishing sacramental policies and procedures in the parish supports these lofty goals of liturgical renewal. Sacramental policies and procedures might address questions like, How do we celebrate these rites in the way the universal church intended? What do we do when it is not possible to celebrate the rites as they are given? How do we establish an order or pastoral practice in our parish that legitimately accommodates the rites to the community's needs? What options do we have for pastoral adaptation? How does a community take responsibility for the way in which the liturgy is celebrated? What is expected of those who preside and preach? What do Catholics have a right to expect from the liturgy?

Closely related to the actual celebration of the liturgy is the preparation and formation of the faithful for the liturgy and the sacraments. Here, the catechetical and liturgical components of pastoral life work hand in hand.

The *Rite of Christian Initiation of Adults* is probably the best example of how evangelization and catechesis lead to liturgy, and liturgy to catechesis. How personal conversion is the foundation upon which catechesis builds is clear in the *Rite of Christian Initiation of Adults*. Catechesis in turn leads us to the liturgy. The liturgy then not only celebrates the stages of conversion, evoked by evangelization and catechesis, but opens the door to further catechesis, which enlightens the experience of the mysteries we celebrate. Consequently, it is not surprising that in formulating sacramental policies and procedures we should also consider their catechetical and formational components.

Some may initially find this discussion about establishing parish sacramental policies and procedures puzzling. After all, they might ask, aren't the rites already prescribed for us? Aren't we bound to the universal liturgical norms and laws governing sacramental life? The answer to these questions, of course, is yes. But the matter is not as simple as it may first appear. There are at least three reasons why this is so.

1. *The rites provide numerous pastoral options.*

The *Order of Christian Funerals*, for example, provides several rites that can be used on the occasion of the death of a Catholic. Whereas the vigil service, the funeral Mass and the committal are the three major pieces, there are other rites, such as prayers at the time of the first viewing of the body. When should these options be used? Who is responsible for making those decisions? Who will preside at which rites? Which rites have priority, and when?

Another example is found in the *Rite of Christian Initiation of Adults*. There are blessings, minor exorcisms and presentations that may be used at various times in the initiation process. When should they be used? by whom? for whom? Which options are appropriate for catechumens but might not be appropriate for baptized candidates?

Yet another example is the *Order of Penance*, which provides three basic formats for celebrating the sacrament of penance and contains sample penitential services. Which format is most appropriate, and how should that be decided? When would a nonsacramental penitential service be appropriate? How can these official rituals be adapted to the parish's needs?

2. *The rites and canons regarding sacramental life are not always specific about how something is to be done.*

The *Rite of Christian Initiation of Adults* states that during the period of the catechumenate, there should be celebrations of the word of God, which may be held during catechetical meetings with the catechumens (RCIA, 84). Except for a bare-bones outline, not much else is provided.

A similar example exists in regard to marriage preparation. The *Code of Canon Law* states that pastors are obliged to see that the community provides couples with a "personal preparation for entering marriage so that through such preparation the parties are predisposed toward the holiness and duties of their new state" (canon 1063). But how much preparation is necessary? What does the preparation include? Who decides? Who is responsible for the preparation? If the diocese offers no policies in regard to this, how can a parish go about establishing policies and procedures for addressing the need? If there is a diocesan policy regarding marriage preparation, how will the parish's policy reflect the diocesan norms?

3. *The rites are sometimes very difficult to celebrate as they are prescribed because the conditions are wanting or the resources are lacking.*

This can be a source of great anxiety. What does one do, for example, with the prescription that only one celebration of the Easter Vigil is to take place in each parish, if the parish church is too small to accommodate a very large congregation that desires to celebrate the Vigil? Is it appropriate to celebrate the Vigil twice? What about accommodating different language groups by providing more than one Vigil? What does a pastor do when he has two missions in addition to his parish, and the two missions are too far away to expect those people to gather at the parish's celebration of the Vigil?

Another example is the church's preference for baptism by immersion. It is clear from the rites and legislation of the church that the ideal manner of celebrating baptism is by immersion. Diocesan law may even require parish churches to have an immersion font. What does a community do when it doesn't have a font big enough for immersion and cannot afford to build one? Or perhaps there is not sufficient space for an immersion font. Is there a vision behind the norm that can be met as an interim measure, or at least partially?

The universal church provides the basic laws that govern sacramental practice. Some of these laws are found in the *Code of Canon Law,* and others are found in the rites themselves, either in the *praenotanda* (introductions) or interspersed throughout the liturgical books as *rubrics* (specific instructions usually printed in red). Like canon law, the rubrics and *praenotanda* are true church laws with the same binding force as the canons of the code. Because of the universal scope of the law, however, it is unreasonable to think that the universal law can resolve all the pastoral questions or dilemmas associated with the application of the law in every parish around the world. At times the national conference of bishops may need to formulate additional laws or sacramental policies that make more explicit the intentions of the universal law. In some cases the national conference of bishops may need to seek an indult from the Holy See, which is an approved exception to the universal law. The diocesan bishop also has the authority to issue specific liturgical laws for the diocesan church as long as they do not contradict the universal law.

At the parish level the pastor may issue policies that are mandatory for the parish, provided these policies are in accord with universal and diocesan law (canon 519). Drafting parish policies and procedures can be an effective means of applying universal and diocesan law. Parish policies help make universal and diocesan law more explicit and provide a good order for the parish that fosters unity and good pastoral care.

Issues in this third category will require dialogue with the office of the chancellor, the diocesan worship office and other competent authorities before a solution is achieved and a policy and procedure adopted. Without this kind of consultation, policies and procedures might be written which later create more problems than they were intended to solve.

The Goal of Policies and Procedures

The goal of establishing policies and procedures is to foster a healthy sacramental life that reflects both the spirit and integrity of the church's tradition as well as good pastoral care of the faithful. Policies and procedures can provide an order for the parish so that the community is united in its celebration of faith and is offered the best possible conditions to experience the full impact of the mysteries that are celebrated.

Policies and procedures also can be a source of support to pastoral ministers charged with making local decisions. Given the guidance, options and clarity of purpose that policies and procedures can provide, pastoral ministers can confidently exercise their leadership. By providing an order that everyone can rely on, established policies and procedures can reduce the stress and burden of trying to resolve common dilemmas or problems each time they occur.

Those charged with drafting policies and procedures will do well if they ask themselves whether their proposals will help foster the spirit of the liturgical renewal as it is envisioned in the *Constitution on the Sacred Liturgy* and subsequent documents on the liturgy. More precisely, to foster liturgical renewal is to enable the community to worship in such a way that the faithful can experience the presence of God in their midst and so be drawn into the divine encounter.

Sometimes the policies and procedures will simply be a reiteration of already mandated universal or diocesan legislation. The policies and procedures may be issued so that they are more easily accessible or because they have a particularly high value for the parish or diocese and need to be emphasized.

The ultimate or sole purpose of policies and procedures ought not be corrective, that is, issued because of neglect or abuse and intended to correct errors. There may indeed need to be corrections, but if this is the driving force behind the policies and procedures, the work will not achieve its full potential. When the motivation for drafting policies and procedures flows from immediate anger, frustration or contempt, the policies risk being cast in a negative or punitive tone. This in turn may make the policies and procedures so unappealing that they might be disregarded by those who were expected to use them.

Lex Orandi, Lex Credendi: What the church prays is what the church believes.

One of the ways the church has traditionally spoken of the value of ritual prayer is to appeal to the ancient principle *lex orandi, lex credendi*. This is loosely translated as "what the church prays is what the church believes."

This means that when we celebrate the liturgy, we publicly demonstrate our faith as Catholics. We reveal our identity. The handing on of the Creed and Lord's Prayer in the *Rite of Christian Initiation of Adults* is a beautiful expression of what the church does in all its liturgical acts. The faith of the church is passed on to us in the praying and doing of the ritual.

All of the ritual books contain rubrics and pastoral notes that are intended to preserve the creed that is embodied in the rite and intended to preserve the unity of believers held together by a common ritual. Granted, sometimes the rubrics might appear a bit obscure or awkward. But there is always a reason these rubrics were deemed necessary. Before dismissing the rubric or making what may be an unnecessary pastoral adaptation, one first needs to discern the value behind the law. When a legitimate adaptation might be necessary, the goal is to maintain the value behind the law or rubric that is adapted.

Not all rubrics have the same weight. Prescribing bread and wine for eucharist, for example, obviously holds more weight than whether the assembly kneels or stands for the eucharistic prayer. Nevertheless, even lesser matters should not be disregarded. Collectively the rubrics hold together a common vision. A common discipline gives shape to a communal life.

Failing to respect the ritual pattern and the rubrics or laws governing sacramental life runs the risk of imposing one's own personal spirituality on the assembly. Pastoral leaders, especially presiders, have a difficult balance to achieve. On the one hand, their faith should give life to their pastoral decisions and their leadership at prayer. On the other hand, their own personal style of prayer and individual spirituality cannot take precedence over the universal church's spirituality and sacramental vision. This is why the *Constitution on the Sacred Liturgy* says that unless "the pastors themselves are thoroughly imbued with the spirit and power of the liturgy," the goals of liturgical reform will not be realized (CSL, 14).

There are limits to applying the principle of *lex orandi, lex credendi* to policies and procedures. The purpose of the liturgy and of the laws that govern it are not only to hold a community together and to pass on truth or doctrine. That in itself would be insufficient. The liturgy is intended to draw us more deeply into the awesome mystery of God. It is this encounter with God that most Catholics desire above all else, even if they are not able to express their need in these terms. Unmet expectations at this level lead many out the door, never to return. Many Catholics who have chosen to absent themselves from worship have done so not because they were upset about an unclear presentation of the truth or an imprecise doctrinal formulation in the prayers, homily or ritual action. They have given up on worship because their longing for God was not satisfied in the liturgy.

There is a need then for balance in addressing policies and procedures. We need to be careful not to fall into the trap of thinking of liturgy as a prepackaged tradition that is handed down intact and into which we are somehow supposed to fit our lives. Liturgy is a living and thus changing tradition that is shaped as much by sensitivity to the human element as it is by the unchanging truth of doctrine and creed. Policies and procedures serve as instruments that preserve the tradition while at the same time respecting and adapting it to the growing and changing human condition.

Can policies and procedures guarantee that our rituals will be an orthodox expression of faith and provide a genuine encounter with God? There is no guarantee, of course. Policies and procedures are but one means of guarding the integrity of our worship and establishing the optimum conditions in which the divine encounter can happen.

Caution! All of this can sound as if sacramental life is entirely dependent on the human component. It is not: We must humbly recognize the free gift of God's grace at work in all of this and without which all our pastoral efforts would be in vain.

"I'm not convinced we need policies and procedures."

Even with all the above said, there may be some who still fail to see the value of issuing policies and procedures. The very mention of the word "law" or "policy" might trigger a negative reaction or be heard as something restrictive or punitive. Our personal history of law and policies can affect us more than we realize; sometimes we have to seek a fresh outlook.

There are some for whom policies and procedures will be received as burdensome or as something that disregards the unique character and needs of their community. This can happen, for instance, in a large but very diverse diocese. It is difficult to provide policies and procedures that can be applied to all the details of every parish. Some will feel imposed upon, disrespected, offended, angered and so on because they feel the policies and procedures are unreasonable or too difficult to implement. What may be lacking in these situations is time taken to study the policies and procedures carefully and to draw out from them the vision and purpose behind them. It is often possible to maintain the value and vision behind the policy even when adaptation or dispensation may be the only recourse.

Perhaps the most common and serious objection to policies and procedures comes from those who feel that policies and procedures are unnecessary: "We know our community best and so we will do what we think is best for us." Being part of the larger Catholic tradition and universal communion might not be highly valued, or this reaction may be the result of the community's past experience of not being given a voice in establishing the policies it was expected to observe.

A still more common objection is to judge policies and procedures as liturgical nit-picking or as something that does not really matter to people. "What difference does it make if we baptize by immersion or use a cupful of water? Isn't either method valid?" "What difference does it make if we have music at Mass or not?" "What difference does it make whether we have a Mass, a communion service or Morning Prayer, as long as the people gather to pray?"

There is, to be sure, a need for balance in these matters. Strict rubrical correctness is not sufficient for building a community of faith. One can fulfill all the external prescriptions of the rites and still not celebrate them as they were intended. And what is more tragic is that the community might go home feeling that the liturgy of the church has nothing to offer them. But the *manner* of the celebration *does* have an effect on us. The effect of the liturgy may be subtle or hard to describe, but it is something that is cumulative over time and so is not just based on our judgment of what occurred on one occasion.

One must also admit, finally, that sometimes policies and procedures are not well drafted or are simply not helpful. When appropriate consultation takes place as part of the drafting process, many of the negative reactions to the policies and procedures can be avoided. At other times, we are faced with policies and procedures that are outdated and unworkable. These have to be reviewed carefully and amended while working within the appropriate structures of authority. The purpose of this book is to facilitate and guide the process of drafting new policies and procedures, and to guide the process of reviewing existing ones in an effective, legitimate and wise pastoral manner.

Those who embark on the difficult task of formulating new policies and procedures or revising old ones will discover that the process itself will be as important as the finished product. The process forces us to review the assumptions we carry deep inside us regarding ritual and sacramental life. The process leads us back to the primary sources to review the church's vision and understanding of the sacraments and provides an appropriate opportunity to assess our pastoral practice in light of the church's discipline and teaching. This will contribute to the ongoing work of liturgical renewal and the revival of sacramental life in our Catholic communities.

■ Parish Work Group Exercise

This exercise is best done with a parish working group. It also can be completed by an individual and then later shared in a group process. The purpose of this exercise is not to produce anything but to aid in the formation of a policy-making committee. These questions may help you begin the process. Feel free to write your reflections on page 11.

1. What are my assumptions about liturgy and sacramental life?

   What value do I see in celebrating the liturgy?

   What connections do the liturgy and the sacraments have to my daily Christian life?

   How does our celebration of the liturgy and the sacraments reflect the identity and beliefs of our community?

   Is our parish's commitment to liturgy and sacramental life reflected in the parish mission statement?

2. What are my attitudes about church law? about sacramental policies and procedures?

3. How are policies arrived at in our parish?

4. Where would I find our parish's sacramental policies and procedures?

5. Where would I find the resources necessary for research on policies and procedures (for example, the *Code of Canon Law*, the rites of the church, diocesan policies)?

6. How might parish sacramental policies and procedures help foster ongoing liturgical renewal in our community?

Interpreting and Applying Policies and Procedures

Because existing policies and procedures are often the catalysts for creating new parish policies and procedures, let us put aside for the moment the need to create new policies and look at how we might interpret and apply existing policies and procedures.

I. *The first stage in interpreting and applying existing policies and procedures is to collect them and begin arranging them in some reasonable order.*

There may already be some existing sacramental policies and procedures in the parish or in the diocese, which in turn affect the parish. However, these policies and procedures may not be found under one cover. They may have been issued at various times and through various means of communication; some may only have been issued orally. It is not uncommon for those concerned to not even be aware of existing policies or procedures in regard to particular issues.

In the parish, the pastoral staff or ad hoc policy committee might be asked to collect and collate all written and unwritten parish sacramental policies and procedures, plus any diocesan policies and procedures that were issued for parish use. On the diocesan level, the chancellor's office and the office for worship may be the two lead agents to consult with in collating existing policies and procedures.

II. *The second stage in interpreting and applying policies and procedures requires understanding the terminology that is used.*

Words like policies, guidelines, mandates, norms, directives, rules, principles, procedures, recommendations, and so on are often used interchangeably to refer to what we are addressing here as policies and procedures. It is not uncommon to find that the terminology is inconsistent even within the same document. In order to interpret the weight or intention of a policy, one needs to understand how the terminology is being used.

Sometimes a diocese or parish uses the word *guideline* when what it really intends is a *policy. Guideline* has the connotation of being a suggestion, not something mandatory. One is not obligated to adhere to guidelines.

In this book the use of the word *policy* has an obligatory character. It obliges those for whom it was written. The policies of the diocesan church are true laws when they are promulgated by decree of the diocesan bishop, who is the sole legislator within the diocese (canon 391.2). Although a pastor is not a legislator, he can use his pastoral authority to issue policies that are mandatory for the parish, provided that the policies are in accord with universal and particular law (canon 519).

Issuing policies by legitimate authority does not imply that the authority has to be exercised unilaterally as a dictatorship. Later we will discuss how policy can be effectively formulated through consultation.

The point being made here is that policies, as we will use the term, are mandatory in nature. The key words often found in policies are *shall* and *will* rather than *should* or *could. Procedures,* as we will use the term, refers to the way in which the policy is to be carried out. Procedures make the policy specific. They tell us how the policy is to be enacted.

In interpreting or reviewing policies and procedures, then, we need to ascertain whether what is presented is in fact a policy or is a guideline or recommendation. Is the terminology consistent? Who do we go to for clarification? Is this policy and/or procedure still in effect? Does it require us to do anything, or does it just grant permission to do something if needed? These are a few of the questions we need to ask when we try to interpret policies and procedures. Most questions about the weight of a policy are the result of inconsistent language. When there is doubt, approaching the lawgiver is the best solution. When that is not possible, the diocesan office of the chancellor and the diocesan worship office may be of assistance.

Let us take an example from the sacramental policies and procedures of the archdiocese of Chicago:

204.2.1 Policy *Auxiliary ministers of communion at Mass shall receive adequate catechesis and liturgical training before they are mandated to exercise their ministry.*

It is clear from this policy that catechesis and liturgical training are mandatory. Notice the use of the word *shall*. This is not guideline language, but mandatory language. Each parish is required to implement this policy within the parish community. The policy does not define what is adequate, nor does it dictate how or by whom adequate preparation and liturgical training should be provided. This is what the parish will need to develop. The procedures that follow the policy must clarify what is expected by the policy and must provide recommendations for keeping it.

Procedures

a) Catechesis and liturgical training for auxiliary ministers of communion at Mass is provided by the local community.

b) Catechesis should include an appreciation for one's baptism and solidarity with the church, an understanding of the eucharist, and an understanding of the significance of this extraordinary ministry.

c) The auxiliary minister's liturgical training should include very specific instruction on the order and practice of distributing Holy Communion in the community.

d) Assistance for catechesis and liturgical training is available through the Office for Divine Worship.

e) Every community is responsible for the formation and spiritual enrichment of mandated communion ministers.

Procedures b and c provide an outline of the basic points to be covered in a training course. Notice, however, that while these procedures spell out in more detail what is expected by the policy, the parish will need to expand on these procedures and make them still more specific.

Another example of how policies and procedures work hand in hand is Policy 301.2.2, regarding the place where the sacrament of penance is celebrated.

301.2.2 Policy *Every parish church and place of worship must make provision for at least one reconciliation room.*

The use of the word *must* clearly makes this more than a recommendation or a guideline. If it said *should*, for example, it could mean that this is a strong recommendation but is not required. There might have been room, then, for an exception.

One might conservatively interpret "reconciliation room" to mean the old confessional. However, the procedure that follows makes it quite clear that a separate room which can accommodate penitents either behind a screen or face-to-face is mandatory.

Procedures

A reconciliation room is, by definition, a physical setting which provides the penitent with all the options of the Rite. It should be of appropriate size and provide a table for the scriptures and a kneeler and screen, as well as a chair for face-to-face confession. Attention should be given to proper lighting, ventilation, acoustics and liturgical symbols. It is not to be used for any purpose other than the celebration of the sacraments.

This procedure makes it quite clear that an old confessional will not suffice because it does not make provision for face-to-face confession. The procedure also gives a fuller description of what that reconciliation room might look like. Given the mandate to provide a reconciliation room, then, a parish could take this procedure as a starting point in creating a reconciliation room or evaluating its present arrangement. The parish might also choose to establish a policy on how confessions will be heard at a communal celebration of the sacrament of penance, at which there may be a need for more than one reconciliation room.

A final example of the importance of terminology and the employment of procedures following a policy is Policy 202.10.2. This policy addresses the issue of daily Mass, particularly in regard to those situations in which there is only one priest in the parish. Parishes that struggle with scheduling are often unsure about what is permissible or appropriate. The following policy establishes the norm upon which the local parish can make a decision about the frequency of daily Mass.

202.10.2 Policy *For a just cause, when there is only one priest assigned to a parish it is permissible to regularly eliminate Mass on one of the weekdays. When a priest is ill or must absent himself from the parish for several days, for example for a retreat, clergy convocation or vacation, there is no obligation to provide the daily Mass.*

What is interesting about this policy is that it does not mandate any action. It simply allows for the possibility of eliminating a Mass. A policy like this provides support, if needed, for making a decision to eliminate a Mass on any particular day. Thus the law in its mandatory form strongly backs any community that chooses this option.

The procedures offer some assistance by recommending what a parish might do if eliminating a Mass is deemed necessary.

Procedures

a) The Mass schedules of neighboring parishes ought to be published for the convenience of the faithful.

b) Especially when Mass cannot be celebrated, the faithful should be encouraged to gather for Morning Prayer or Evening Prayer or a Liturgy of the Word.

c) Communion services are permitted in conformity with the principles issued in §206, Weekday Communion Services.

These procedures do not exhaust the possibilities for what a community might do if there is no Mass on a particular weekday. What is listed under procedures becomes the starting point for the parish in creating its own list of procedures.

III. *A third stage in interpreting and applying existing policies and procedures is understanding the particular values that are embodied in the policies and procedures.*

Why was this policy written? What were the drafters of this policy and its procedures hoping to preserve as a value? Was there something specific that occasioned this policy? What is the local history behind it? What do the ritual books have to say about the subject? What are the inherent sacramental principles and values underlying the policies and procedures?

The value behind a particular policy might fall under any number of categories that can help us better understand the intent of the policy:

1. INTRINSIC SACRAMENTAL RUBRIC
2. INTEGRITY OF THE RITE
3. PASTORAL LEADERSHIP AND COMMUNITY RESPONSIBILITY
4. PASTORAL CARE AND THE RIGHTS OF THE FAITHFUL
5. MINISTERIAL EXPECTATIONS AND STANDARDS
6. VISION STATEMENTS

Let us look at each of these categories.

1. INTRINSIC SACRAMENTAL RUBRIC

An *intrinsic sacramental rubric* is one that is essential to the rite itself. In other words, not observing the rubric is not celebrating the ritual. Thus the rubric requiring that bread and wine be used for the eucharist and that the words of the eucharistic prayer be proclaimed over these elements is intrinsic or essential to the rite. Not to observe this rubric means that the church's eucharist was not celebrated.

A less extreme example may be helpful. In the sacramental policies and procedures of the archdiocese of Chicago, Policy 202.8 reiterates the universal church law requiring that the Easter Vigil be celebrated at night. Why at night? What's so terribly wrong about starting the Easter Vigil at 4:30 PM for the convenience of the people? A close examination of the Easter Vigil reveals that the darkness of night is so essential to the celebration of the Vigil that without it, the meaning of the liturgy is obscured. Thus to begin the Service of Light when it is still light outdoors is an anomaly. To hear the cantor sing in the Exultet "most blessed of all nights" would require more imagination than should be necessary.

What is it in our tradition that makes us have such strong feelings about this that a rubric has been mandated for the universal church? What meaning are we to derive from a community gathering in the darkness of night to light a new fire? The affective experience of darkness contrasted with light is so essential to the ritual that one can say it is not possible to celebrate the Service of Light without it.

Still another example of an intrinsic sacramental rubric is the expectation that the committal service from the *Order of Christian Funerals* be celebrated at the *final resting place*. The policy states it this way:

704.2.1 Policy *The committal service shall be celebrated at the place of burial or interment and not at the church (OCF, 204).*

The committal service is the church's ritual prayer surrounding the deeply human experience of leaving the remains of the deceased at his or her *final* resting place. An examination of the texts from the *Order of Christian Funerals* reveals its meaning:

"In sure and certain hope of the resurrection to eternal life through our Lord Jesus Christ, we commend to almighty God our brother/sister N., and we commit his/her body to the ground, earth to earth, ashes to ashes, dust to dust" (OCF, 219).

Our emotions at the church at the end of a funeral Mass are different from what we feel, at least in matter of degree, in the physical act of leaving the body behind at the cemetery. An observation of human behavior will reveal that this final leave-taking at the cemetery is often the most emotional experience in the panoply of rites at the death of a Christian. The committal rite tries to capture the reality of these emotions at this significant turning point through prayer, song and the physical act of leaving the remains behind.

Using the committal rite at the doors of the church simply does not fulfill the purpose of the committal because that is not the final resting place. The rubric determining the place of the ritual is intrinsic, then, to the ritual itself.

2. INTEGRITY OF THE RITE

The integrity of a rite is very closely aligned to the intrinsic sacramental rubric. Rubrics or policies in this category are prescribed so that the rite will be celebrated in such a way that we are able to experience the optimum effect of the rite itself. While validity is not an issue here, the proper use of the signs and symbols of the liturgy is very important if we expect them to effect what they truly signify.

Policy 103.10.1, regarding the manner of baptizing, may be a helpful example. It is a direct quote from the U.S. National Statutes regarding Christian initiation.

103.10.1 Policy *Baptism by immersion is the fuller and more expressive sign of the sacrament and, therefore, provision should be made for its more frequent use in the baptism of adults. The provision of the* Rite of Christian Initiation of Adults *for partial immersion, namely, immersion of the candidate's head, should be taken into account (National Statutes, 17).*

What is the value of immersion? We know that even if only a cupful of water is poured over the head, the baptism is valid. So why immersion?

A worthy, meaningful and effective celebration of the sacrament of baptism requires more than validity. Of course, a person baptized by infusion (pouring) is validly baptized, but the power of the sign is greatly diminished when only a small cup of water is used, baptismal images of creation and the flood, of the waters that saved Israel in exodus, of the waters of the Jordan, of the water flowing from the side of Christ crucified — all these are powerful images that are hard to imagine when the symbolic act is impoverished. Paul preached to the Romans: "Are you not aware that when you were baptized you died with Christ?" (See Romans 6:3) It is hard to connect Paul's powerful baptismal image to a celebration in which only a small cup of water is used.

Policies that are written to preserve the integrity of the rite itself, then, are not superfluous to the sacramental act. By their nature, the sacraments rely upon human, physical and tactile matter to effect what they signify. When this is neglected, the integrity of the rite is at risk and we have a less than full sacramental experience. (For other examples in this category, see Policy 301.2.2, regarding the sacrament of penance, or Policy 404.15.1, regarding music for the Rite of Marriage.)

3. PASTORAL LEADERSHIP AND COMMUNITY RESPONSIBILITY

The values that fall under this category give direction for how ministry is to function within the community. While pastoral leadership is responsible for coordinating and directing parish ministries, the whole parish is called to pastor one another responsibly . The *Rite of Christian Initiation of Adults* states emphatically that the initiation of new Christians is the responsibility of all the baptized (RCIA, 9). The *Order of Christian Funerals* speaks about the ministry of consolation entrusted to the community (OCF, 9).

An example of how these principles regarding pastoral leadership and community responsibility are put into policy is found in the following policy regarding collaboration in initiation ministry:

102.1.1 Policy *Because the initiation of adults is "the responsibility of all the baptized" (RCIA, 9), pastors shall associate with themselves men and women of the parish who, as catechists, sponsors, and in other roles, collaborate with them in the formation and initiation of new members. It is the pastor's responsibility to see that those who assist in the initiation process have been properly trained.*

Another example in this category is the community's responsibility for preparing engaged couples for marriage:

401.1.1 Policy *The parish community shall take responsibility for preparing couples not only for their wedding day but for the lifetime commitment of living a Christian marriage.*

These policies were written to ensure that the baptized not only are invited by the pastor to share in the pastoral ministry but also are expected to do so by virtue of their baptism.

4. PASTORAL CARE AND THE RIGHTS OF THE FAITHFUL

Under this category belong those rights that a Catholic should be able to claim as a member of the baptized faithful. One could say that these are the things Catholics are entitled to or should expect as part of the pastoral care the church provides.

For example, Policy 701.1.1 states that every Catholic is entitled to the church's ministry at the time of death. It would seem that this is a given assumption in parish life. However, unusual circumstances surrounding a person's death sometimes raise questions about appropriate pastoral care. Thus, for instance, there might be some cases in which a Catholic might not be granted a funeral Mass because of public scandal. And what do we do when someone requests burial for a relative who was not a parishioner and did not belong to any parish? Notice that the policy does not state how the church's ministry is extended to the family of the deceased. The policy-makers in the parish will need to be specific in interpreting this policy so that when the occasion arises, they will be prepared to deal with it.

Another example in this category is the requirement for marriage preparation. The following policy requires at minimum a four-month period of preparation:

401.2.1 Policy *The formal preparation for marriage shall begin at least four months before the anticipated date of the wedding.*

According to this policy, not only do Catholics have a right to pre-marriage pastoral care, they have a responsibility to accept this as part of the necessary preparation for Christian married life.

(For other examples in this category, see Policy 101.3.2, regarding sacramental preparation of parents for the baptism of their infant; Policy 202.16.1, regarding the need for parishes to provide access for the elderly and people with disabilities; Policy 201.2.1, regarding the faithful's right and duty to participate fully in the celebration of Mass; and Policy 106.5.1, which states catechumens' right to Christian burial.)

5. MINISTERIAL EXPECTATIONS AND STANDARDS

Under this category we find the values that ensure that the ministries will be performed in a professional manner. Here we will find issues regarding presiding, ministerial formation and clerical faculties.

204.6.1 Policy *Auxiliary ministers of communion at Mass or for the sick may preside at a public communion service, provided they have been properly trained and have received the special mandate to preside at these services.*

This policy and the procedures that follow it are intended to establish some criteria for competence. In addition to the training requirement, note that a special mandate is required to exercise this ministry. This additional expectation emphasizes the value of these ministers being specially prepared. It should be obvious from the requirements listed that the archdiocese of Chicago places a great deal of importance on the role of presiding. While the structure of the training may vary, it should be clear from this policy that training cannot be dismissed.

Another example of a policy that embodies ministerial expectations and standards is Policy 202.17.1. It is a repetition of canons 905.1 and 905.2. It indicates that "for a just cause, a priest is permitted to celebrate Mass twice on any given day, . . . a third Mass on Sundays." This policy underscores what is expected of the priest and details his faculties. The purpose of a policy such as this may be to establish the ground for making a new parish Mass schedule. If the parish priest can celebrate only a certain number of Masses on a Sunday, then this policy will need to be taken into account as the number of Masses to be scheduled is considered.

(For another example under this category, see Policy 702.4.1, regarding presiding at funeral rites.)

6. VISION STATEMENTS

In this category we find some policies and procedures that might sound rather obvious or strike us as terribly idealistic. But the intent of policies and procedures that contribute toward a vision statement is to articulate a direction for sacramental life even if the full implementation of the policy or procedure cannot be immediately realized.

Policy 201.1.1 sounds almost too general to be useful: "The Sunday eucharist requires the utmost care in preparation and celebration." Upon further reflection, one would naturally inquire as to how that care in preparation and celebration will be assured. How is it to be measured? Who is responsible for it? This policy is actually very strong in that it makes the liturgy such a high priority. The parish policies and procedures that will reflect this policy will make all the difference in whether this vision statement becomes a pious admonition or becomes the guiding force in the parish community.

Another example in this category tries to further the practice of praying the Liturgy of the Hours. Read carefully the way the following policy is stated:

205.1.1 Policy *Parishes shall catechize the faithful about the importance of daily prayer and promote the daily celebration of at least some part of the Liturgy of the Hours.*

There are two directives to the policy: to catechize the faithful and to celebrate the Liturgy of the Hours. The principle value in this policy is to teach the faithful about the importance of daily prayer. The way the policy is written, though, tells us that we are not necessarily expected to immediately schedule daily Morning Prayer, Evening Prayer and Night Prayer. What there is here is encouragement to begin acquainting the community with the church's daily prayer. This policy then becomes a vision statement that provides us with some direction. Each parish will have much work to do in determining how to implement this policy. (For another example in this category see Policy 404.2.1, regarding the assembly's participation at weddings.)

IV. *When a policy or procedure is being formally reviewed, the question needs to be raised of whether the policy or procedure is still applicable and is still needed.*

A parish reviewing its own policies and procedures could initiate a consultation process for this purpose before actually revising the policy or procedure, or deleting it. A particular policy or procedure may have been written a long time ago and is now no longer applicable; thus it would simply need to be deleted.

V. *When the parish interprets and applies policies and procedures, it needs to give an honest assessment of how parish practice matches the expectation of the policies and procedures.*

Does parish practice reflect what is found in the policy or procedure? What would it take to bring the parish into conformity with the policy? This is where many key questions will surface that test our assumptions about sacramental practice. In some cases we will be able to offer a good status report. At other times we will have to decide what we need to do to achieve the ideal.

At its best, a process of critical assessment of parish practice will drive us to reflect more deeply on the meaning and significance of the liturgy and the sacraments. When we are not in sync with a particular policy, we will need to ask why this is so. Is there a clash of values or theologies? This critical review can be the most valuable piece in the whole process because it demands a thorough reflection on the meaning and purpose of the sacraments and on how the celebration of these sacraments expresses our beliefs, identity and mission as a Catholic community.

VI. *At this stage, the parish reaches the point of implementation.*

There are five basic categories of questions that accompany the implementation process:

1. Has this policy already been implemented? If not, when will the policy be implemented? An implementation date needs to be set. It could be immediate or it could be delayed so that a proper catechesis may be provided and its implementation communicated to all.

2. How will it be implemented? Will the policy take full effect at once or in stages?

3. How will the policy be communicated to the community? Will the bulletin be used or will there be a town hall meeting? If the policy affects a wide range of people and the matter is of great importance, will a special mailing be required?

4. Who will be responsible for the implementation? This is a crucial question because unless it is clear who is responsible, the full implementation may never occur. The expectations attached to the implementation need to be as clear as possible to the person (or persons) charged with it.

5. How will the effect or success of the implementation be measured? This is an important step in the process so that future policy revisions can be made based on what is learned regarding the policy's feasibility.

Establishing some criteria by which to measure the success of the implementation of policies and procedures can lead to an ongoing process of keeping sacramental policies and procedures up-to-date.

■ Worksheet 1

Take a parish policy (written and published or just observed by oral tradition) and follow the steps outlined in the previous chapter. Use the next few pages to consider this policy closely and answer the questions about it.

PARISH SACRAMENTAL POLICY

_____

_____

_____

_____

_____

_____

_____

_____

_____

1. What does the language in the above documentation tell us about this statement?
   Is this a policy, or is it just a guideline or procedure? Is the language consistent?

2. What are the values underlying this policy?
   Why do you think it was written?
   Can anyone give some background on the origin of this policy?

3. Is this policy still in effect? Is it still needed?

4. Has this policy worked? How does current practice meet the expectations of this policy?

continued

5. Was this policy ever formally implemented? Does it need to be reintroduced to the community? Does it call for fresh catechesis?

_____

_____

_____

_____

_____

_____

_____

_____

_____

_____

_____

_____

_____

_____

_____

_____

_____

_____

_____

_____

_____

_____

■ Worksheet 2

Take a diocesan policy (written and published or just observed by oral tradition) and follow the steps outlined in the previous chapter.

DIOCESAN SACRAMENTAL POLICY

_____

_____

_____

_____

_____

_____

_____

_____

1. What does the language in the above documentation tell us about this statement?
   Is this a policy, or is it just a guideline or procedure?
   Is the language consistent?

2. What are the values underlying this policy?
   Why do you think it was written?
   Who might be able to offer some background on the origin of this policy?

3. Is this policy still in effect? Is it applicable to our community?

continued

4. How has this policy found expression in our parish? Did the parish create a local policy to implement the diocesan policy? How does current parish practice meet the expectations of the diocesan policy?

5. Was this policy or a subsequent parish policy, based on the above, ever formally implemented? Does it need to be reintroduced to the community? Does it call for fresh catechesis?

_____

_____

_____

_____

_____

_____

_____

_____

_____

_____

_____

_____

_____

_____

_____

_____

_____

_____

chapter

III

Drafting Policies and Procedures

The need for sacramental policies and procedures arises from a desire for good pastoral order, a set way of doing things. The need may arise because there has been confusion or disagreement in the past about how the parish responds to given pastoral circumstances. Thus, for example, what does the pastor do when there is a request for a third wedding Mass on a Saturday and he is the only priest available on weekends? Should a decision be made each time the situation arises? Will parishioners cry "unfair" if these situations are handled inconsistently? Would it be easier on the pastoral staff if there were some policies and procedures in place with which they could make pastoral decisions?

The need for sacramental policies and procedures may also arise when the diocese or universal church issues a mandate or law requiring that the parish adopt a new policy into its way of life. The diocesan or universal policy may require a change in the parish's current practice and thus dictate the need for a new parish policy.

The formulation of policies and procedures also may be the result of a longer process of sacramental renewal in which a community systematically, over time, critically reviews the major components of its sacramental life. Thus a parish might begin by reviewing its celebration of the Sunday eucharist and then review each of the sacraments and other key liturgical experiences, such as funerals or the visitation of the homebound with communion. This kind of systematic and comprehensive review will be more valuable than a piecemeal review of sacramental policies and procedures prompted by immediate problems or crises. Allow sufficient time when you're setting down a long-range plan; you don't want to rush the learning potential and the deepening of religious convictions.

A longer-range comprehensive review of sacramental life is what this workbook proposes as the ideal. Far more is involved than producing written policies and procedures — the value of a thorough process is that it can stimulate a renewed understanding and appreciation of the liturgy and the sacraments. The policies and procedures that emerge then will be statements of the community's convictions which support and deeply anchor their renewed appreciation for Catholic sacramental life.

In every case, drafting policies and procedures flows from a parish's understanding of itself as church. Whatever policies and procedures may be written, they are a reflection of the parish's self-understanding as a worshiping community and as a particular expression of the universal church. Policies and procedures will embody what the parish values. When followed, the policies and procedures will further shape and strengthen the identity of the parish.

What this implies, therefore, is that before a parish sets out to write policies and procedures, it ought to consider some basic questions about its own life:

- Who are we as [N.] parish?
- What do we value?
- What do we believe about the sacraments and the liturgy in general?
- Who celebrates the sacraments?
- How is our sacramental life connected with everything else we do as a parish?
- How will our policies and procedures relate to our self-understanding?
- How are decisions made in this parish?
- Do we believe in consultation and that the voice of the parishioners is vital in any process leading to policies and procedures?
- Are decisions made by the pastoral council? by the pastoral staff? by the pastor or by some combination of parish decision-making bodies?
- Does the pastor exercise veto power? Is that clear to everyone? How do we understand our relationship to the diocesan church and the universal church?
- What responsibility do we have to maintain our communion with the larger church?

All of these questions may appear academic at first. But unless these questions can be answered clearly, the process of drafting policies and procedures may only be a confusing and frustrating exercise.

The steps in the process:

1. Choosing the policy-making committee
2. Assessing the situation
3. Reviewing existing legislation
4. Identifying the values at stake
5. Brainstorming for options and solutions
6. Prioritizing the options and possible solutions
7. Seeking further consultation and research (optional)
8. Formulating a draft
9. Reviewing the draft, editing the draft, accepting the draft
10. Implementing the policies and procedures
11. Evaluating the effectiveness of the policies and procedures

For purposes of studying how the above steps can be applied, let us look at the hypothetical 2500-household parish of St. Stephen. There is only one priest assigned to the parish; he is assisted by a deacon. The parish averages 60 funerals and 75 weddings annually. The weekend liturgy schedule includes a Saturday morning Mass at 8:00 AM, the sacrament of penance from 4:00 PM to 4:45 PM, and a Saturday evening Mass at 5:00 PM. The pastor has raised the question of how many weddings the parish should schedule on any given Saturday. Because there is only one priest assigned to the parish, the pastor feels there has to be a limit. Let us consider this situation by following the steps listed above.

1. *Choosing the policy-making committee*

Given the pastoral situation at hand, who should be involved in addressing this pastoral concern? Ordinarily the pastoral council has been the decision-making body at St. Stephen, with the pastor holding veto power. But because the issue of the number of Saturday weddings would involve the parish musician, the couples on the marriage preparation team and the deacon, the pastoral council may recommend that these other relevant parties be invited to participate in the policy-making process. Or the pastoral council may recommend that an ad hoc committee be convened consisting of representatives from the council and other relevant persons.

Because the work of policy making is difficult and tedious, there may be a case for establishing a permanent parish policy-making board. In some sense, one could speak of a special vocation for policy making. Given the gifts and expertise that policy making requires, a special policy-making board may serve the parish well if, of course, it is committed to consulting with other bodies in the parish. Individuals who have a good sense of the church's basic teachings, an ability to read and study church documentation and a facility with language can be invited to become part of a policy-making committee. Often there are parishioners who in their daily work have experience with policy making.

With any policy-making body, there is always a need for education, both in the process of policy and decision making and in regard to whatever issue is being addressed. Without this education or formation, the risk of frustration, misunderstanding and ineffectiveness is much greater.

Let us assume that our hypothetical example of St. Stephen parish has chosen to establish an ad hoc committee to work on this issue and to bring a policy proposal to the full council for review and approval. Let us also assume that they have chosen to involve the parish musician, the deacon, the chair of the liturgy committee and the couple who coordinate the marriage preparation team. The ad hoc committee will choose their own chair, who will facilitate meetings. Because the pastor is personally involved in the issue raised, it is wisely decided that he should not chair the committee.

2. *Assessing the situation*

In assessing the situation it will be important to have an accurate account of how many weddings and funerals were celebrated on every Saturday during the past twelve months. How many of the weddings were nuptial Masses? How many wedding celebrations did the deacon preside at? A review of the entire Saturday liturgy schedule also would be in order. For example, what is the attendance at the 8:00 AM Mass? What is the current parish scheduling policy for weddings? Is there a policy?

The pastor, who raised the issue, needs to be clear about what he believes the problem is. For example, is it a personal problem for him because he feels the burden of presiding at too many Masses? Is it a problem for the parish musician, who is expected to play at all these weddings? Is it a scheduling and space problem? He needs to articulate the problem so that in the course of the discussions that will follow, the committee does not lose sight of why they were convened.

In this hypothetical situation we will assume that the pastor has identified the number of liturgies celebrated on Saturday as the major concern. He feels overburdened by the number of Masses he is expected to celebrate; it has not been uncommon for him to preside at five Masses on a Saturday.

3. *Reviewing existing legislation*

Reviewing existing legislation means looking at what might be the parish's current policy, whether written or oral. It also means reviewing any diocesan or universal legislation that may impinge upon the issue. This review is important so that the parish does not proceed to draft policies and procedures that later are found to be in contradiction to legislation issued by a higher authority.

As St. Stephen parish addresses their pastoral concern, they might study the following policies and procedures taken from Chicago's sacramental policies and procedures.

202.17.1 Policy *For a just cause, a priest is permitted to celebrate Mass twice on any given day. If pastoral necessity requires, he is permitted to celebrate a third Mass on Sundays and holy days of obligation.*

403.1.1 Policy *A parish, through consultation with the parish pastoral council and the liturgy committee, may develop a policy restricting the number of weddings on a given day, depending on the pastoral situation and the number of ministers available to celebrate marriages. This parish policy also includes the scheduling of special wedding anniversary Masses.*

Procedures

a) Church law (canon 905) expressly prohibits priests celebrating more than one Mass a day except in those cases where the law permits multiple celebrations. This law allows the ordinary to permit a priest to celebrate two Masses on a weekday and three Masses on a Sunday or holy day. The ordinary does not have the authority to permit more Masses to be celebrated by an individual priest.

b) If a parish has a large number of weddings, after reviewing the week-end Mass schedule in consultation with the parish pastoral council and the liturgy committee, it is possible to eliminate the Saturday morning Mass.

c) When the Mass in which the sacrament of marriage is celebrated is a regular parish Sunday Mass, the Mass of the day is celebrated.

In addition to the above legislation, the committee would be wise to review what canon law prescribes and what might be found in the Rite of Marriage. Sometimes the documentation that needs to be referred to goes beyond official church documentation. The writings or commentaries of respected authors on related issues can be quite helpful, especially as the working committee tries to interpret the church's documentation. Also, secular material may be useful. If the issue is accessibility for people with disabilities, for example, knowing the city codes might be essential to the decision-making process. Or if a new baptismal font is being installed, some construction or architectural information may be useful.

4. *Identifying the values at stake*

Before discussing solutions to pastoral issues, it is important to identify what underlying values are at stake. Otherwise, solutions might be proposed that do not adequately address the concern. For the committee to proceed effectively together in solidarity, it is important for everyone to be clear about the values that need to be preserved.

In our hypothetical case of St. Stephen, the primary value at stake may be a commitment to good worship. The pastor may argue that by the time he celebrates a third Mass, he is not able to preside with much energy or preach with much enthusiasm. Thus the quality of the liturgy goes down. An equally important value might be the belief that all parishioners should have the opportunity to celebrate their marriage at Mass.

5. *Brainstorming for options and solutions*

After following the above steps, the committee may be ready to discuss the issue more broadly and to brainstorm for options and possible solutions. At this phase of the process it should be stated clearly that the committee is only brainstorming for options and possible solutions — it is not yet making decisions. It would also be helpful to let everyone have an opportunity to propose their ideas without much discussion or argument until after everyone has had an opportunity to share their proposals.

Let us imagine that at St. Stephen the following ideas were proposed:

- Eliminate the Saturday morning Mass.
- Do not allow nuptial Masses.
- Find another priest to assist the pastor.
- Allow only one nuptial Mass every Saturday.
- Encourage celebrating weddings at the Saturday evening Mass.
- Make provision for two wedding Masses and two wedding ceremonies to be celebrated.
- Refuse to schedule weddings for people who are not registered parishioners of the parish.

Once everyone has had an opportunity to list their ideas, discussion would begin. Some ideas would need to be deleted at the start because they conflict with church law. For example, the parish cannot refuse to marry a couple if one or both parties live within the parish territory, even if they are not registered.

Other ideas simply might not be reasonable. For example, it might not be possible to find a priest who could assist the pastor.

It is important to note here that at times a policy is not necessary. Sometimes an action statement will be sufficient. This is especially true if the issue that needs to be resolved is a one-time occasion. Thus if the parish church always has not had enough seating during the summer months, the committee could simply make an action statement that authorizes the pastor to purchase movable chairs and use them during the summer. On the other hand, if an issue is recurring and will continue to raise questions from the congregation, a written policy is more permanent and can be referred to directly. Thus it might be decided that during Lent, the parish will not celebrate baptisms or weddings. A written and approved policy would be more advantageous because it can be published and can be of interest every year.

6. *Prioritizing the options and possible solutions*

After sufficient discussion, the committee should prioritize the options and possible solutions. Which of the suggestions have the strongest appeal to the majority?

At St. Stephen, let us presume that the committee prioritized the suggestions as follows:

1. Eliminate the Saturday morning Mass.
2. Make provision for two wedding Masses and two wedding ceremonies.
3. Encourage celebrating weddings at the Saturday evening Mass.

Although these are the ideas the committee chose to pursue further, this doesn't mean that these ideas might not be altered as the process continues. The decision at this point has been to further unfold the potential for each of the ideas.

7. *Seeking further consultation and research (optional)*

Let us presume that the committee has chosen to extend the consultation process by seeking the advice of couples who were married recently or are about to be married. Consultation might also have been extended to the regular Saturday morning Mass participants.

8. *Formulating a draft*

Having completed all the above steps, the committee is now ready to formulate a draft of a policy. Because the writing of a document is difficult to accomplish as a committee, one or two individuals should be delegated to prepare the draft. The draft should incorporate as best as possible the ideas and recommendations of the whole committee. It ought to reflect the spirit of the discussion process and ought to be especially sensitive to the values the committee enunciated.

9. *Reviewing the draft, editing the draft, accepting the draft*

Once a draft has been prepared, it should be sent to committee members in advance of reconvening the group. This will allow the committee to study the draft carefully before meeting to review and edit it. At the committee meeting, necessary changes can be made. Care should be taken that changes in wording or phrasing do not become a major point of argumentation and take up too much valuable meeting time. When the process reaches this kind of snag but the choices in wording would not alter the content, it is better for the facilitator to note the recommendations and clarify the value that needs to be maintained. An editor can then incorporate these recommendations outside the committee's meeting time.

Let us presume that the committee has finally agreed to the following policies and procedures:

Policy 1 *St. Stephen Parish will celebrate Saturday Morning Prayer at 8:00 AM every Saturday with the distribution of Holy Communion.*

Procedures

a) Although St. Stephen parish does not offer a Saturday morning Mass, parishioners are invited to celebrate the Eucharist at any of the weddings or funerals celebrated on Saturday.

b) St. Michael parish offers a Saturday Mass at 7:30 AM. St. Stephen parishioners are welcome to attend.

Policy 2 *St. Stephen parish will offer four set times for wedding celebrations. The parish shall schedule no more than two wedding Masses on any Saturday.*

Procedures

a) Weddings at St. Stephen Parish may be scheduled for any of the following four set times: 11:00 AM, 12:30 PM, 2:00 PM and 3:30 PM. Wedding times are scheduled on a first come, first serve basis.

b) Because the parish is only able to schedule two wedding Masses on any given Saturday, the wedding Masses are assigned on a first come, first serve basis.

Policy 3 *St. Stephen parish encourages engaged couples to celebrate their wedding at the Saturday evening vigil Mass. St. Stephen parish will celebrate wedding Masses at the Saturday evening vigil Mass whenever it is requested by an engaged couple.*

The proposed policies and procedures appear to address the issues the committee was asked to address. However, a closer examination of these policies and procedures leaves some questions unanswered. For example, Policy 2 does not indicate whether there is an exception to the policy if a visiting priest is scheduled to preside at a wedding. The same policy also does not resolve the issue of bination, namely, that the priest is only able to celebrate two Masses on a Saturday (see Policy 202.17.1 above). Policy 2 also is not clear about the role of the deacon. Does the policy presume that the deacon will preside at all weddings celebrated outside Mass? Or does the policy envision that the pastor may preside at two wedding Masses and then at two weddings celebrated outside of Mass? Does each engaged couple choose the presider? These questions need to be answered in advance.

Policy 3 seems to be reasonable, except in light of our note earlier that the number of weddings averages 75 annually. Does this mean that the Saturday evening Mass could conceivably welcome a wedding celebration on half the weekends of the year? And what about Lent and Advent? Is the parish willing to schedule weddings on these weekends? The result might be that the pastor and the committee are willing to endorse the policy on a trial basis and iron out the difficulties as they arise. Whatever the final decision, it is wise to consider all the possible scenarios so that the parish is prepared to meet the pastoral circumstances as they arise.

Presuming that the editing process is agreed upon, the committee can then approve or reject the policies and procedures. The pastor will then accept or veto the proposals.

10. *Implementing the policies and procedures*

Implementing the policies and procedures is just as important as formulating them. A few of the questions that need to be addressed are: Who will take responsibility for the implementation? How will these new policies and procedures be communicated to the parishioners? Will catechesis be needed? When will these policies and procedures take effect? Where will these polices and procedures be recorded or kept for reference?

11. *Evaluating the policies and procedures*

It would be wise to set a time line for reviewing the effectiveness of the new policies and procedures. If after six months, for example, a review reveals several unforeseen problems, then revisions or adjustments to the policies or procedures can be made. There's not much point to having policies that do not work. Pastoral councils and pastoral staffs should not be discouraged too quickly. It often takes a few revisions to find the best workable solution.

■ Policy-Making Exercise A

Each of these sample exercises begins with a particular issue and its corresponding policy in the Sacramental Policies and Procedures of the Archdiocese of Chicago. *Parish communities can use these exercises to develop their own skills in developing policies. Once the pattern is learned, the subject of each exercise can be changed to whatever issue the parish wishes to address. The "introductory statement of policy" at the beginning of the exercise should include whatever diocesan or universal policies are in place. Where there is no policy to work from, step three, "review of church documentation," may be substituted as the "introductory statement of policy."*

Subject: Easter Vigil

Example of intrinsic sacramental rubric

Introductory statement of policy:

202.8.1 Policy *While it fulfills the Sunday obligation, the Easter Vigil is not to be considered a Mass of anticipation for Easter but a unique liturgical experience in its own right. It shall not be celebrated until it is dark.*

---

1. Who will be involved in addressing this issue?

2. When does our parish celebrate the Easter Vigil?
   How does our parish practice reflect the introductory statement of policy?

continued

3. Review church documentation.

For example, "The entire celebration of the Easter Vigil takes place at night. It should not begin before nightfall; it should end before daybreak on Sunday" (Roman Missal).

For example, "The entire celebration of the Easter Vigil takes place at night, so that it begins after nightfall and ends before dawn. Within this time, that hour is preferable which is most suited to the largest number of people" (Roman Calendar).

4. What values are at stake in this policy?

What values are at stake in the community relative to this policy?

5. What are the obstacles to celebrating the Easter Vigil in the darkness of night?

How can these obstacles be overcome?

What changes in our parish's observance of the Easter Vigil do we need to consider?

What are the options for celebrating the Vigil in conformity with the policy?

6. Prioritize the options.

7. Do we need to consult with anyone else in regard to this issue? For example, what is the practice of celebrating the Vigil at our neighboring parish?

8. Is a written policy necessary? If so, who will prepare a draft?

What process will we use to reach a consensus on the issue or review and approve a policy?

continued

After a draft has been prepared:

9. Does this draft adequately address our concern? Does it need to be edited?

After a draft has been accepted and approved:

10. How will we implement this policy?
What kind of catechesis will we need to offer the parish community?
When?
Who will be responsible for this?

11. How will we judge the effectiveness of this policy?
When will we evaluate the policy?

_____

_____

_____

_____

_____

_____

_____

_____

_____

_____

_____

_____

■ Policy-Making Exercise B

Subject: Rite of Committal

Example of intrinsic sacramental rubric

Introductory statement of policy:

704.2.1 Policy *The committal service shall be celebrated at the place of burial or interment and not at the church (OCF, 204).*

---

1. Who will be involved in addressing this issue?

2. How is the Rite of Committal celebrated in our community?

   Is there an unspoken policy or assumption in the parish regarding committal?

   Is the parish practice in conformity with the above policy statement?

3. Review church documentation and liturgical commentaries.

   For example, "The rite of committal, the conclusion of the funeral rites, is the final act of the community of faith in caring for the body of its deceased member. It may be celebrated at the grave, tomb, or crematorium and may be used for burial at sea. Whenever possible, the rite of committal is to be celebrated at the site of committal, that is, beside the open grave or place of interment, rather than at a cemetery chapel" (OCF, 204).

4. What values are at stake in this policy?

   What values are at stake in the community?

   Do grieving families have some expectations about the funeral rites?

continued

5. If parish practice does not correspond to the above policy, what would it take to change local practice? What are the reasons local parish practice came to be the way it is? What are the options for the future?

6. Prioritize the options and eliminate those that are not feasible.

7. Do we need to consult with anyone else on this matter?
   What are the positions of the cemetery administrations?
   Do we need to consult with funeral directors?

8. Is a written policy necessary for the parish? If so, who will prepare a draft?
   What process will we use to reach a consensus on the issue or review and approve a policy?

After a draft has been prepared:

9. Does the draft reflect the consensus of the policy-making committee?
   Does it need to be edited?

After a draft has been accepted and approved:

10. How will we implement this policy?
    Who needs to be informed about this policy?
    Is the acceptance of this policy an occasion for catechesis on funeral rites?

11. How will we judge the effectiveness of this policy?
    When will we evaluate the policy?

■ Policy-Making Exercise C

Subject: Baptismal font for immersion

Example of integrity of the rite

Introductory statement of policy:

103.10.2 Policy *In the archdiocese of Chicago, whenever a new church is erected, provision must be made for a font that allows for immersion. When a church is renovated, the font should be constructed to allow for the immersion of infants at least, and for the immersion of adults, if possible. (See* Environment and Art in Catholic Worship, *76;* Rite of Baptism for Children, *19, 22;* RCIA, *213;* Catechism of the Catholic Church, *1214, 1239, 1262, 628).*

1. Who will be involved in addressing this issue?

2. How does our parish celebrate infant and adult baptisms?
   Has the parish ever attempted immersion?
   Has this been offered to parents and catechumens as an option?

3. Review church documentation and liturgical commentaries.
   (The recommended readings that are attached to the above policy are a good place to begin this research).

4. What are the theological, liturgical and sacramental values that underlie this policy?

continued

5. Is there resistance to this diocesan policy? Why?

Are there genuine objections to immersion, or is there simply difficulty in imagining how to do it?

Are physical environment issues at stake?

Financial concerns?

What options can we consider?

6. Prioritize the options.

7. Who else do we need to consult with? the diocesan worship office? neighboring parishes? an architect or liturgical design consultant?

8. Is a written policy necessary? If so, who will prepare a draft? What is the timeline for making a decision on this matter? Would an action statement rather than a policy be more appropriate in this case? For example, could the committee recommend to the pastoral council and the pastor that the parish pursue making provision for an immersion font?

After a draft has been prepared:

9. Does this draft adequately address our concern? Does it need to be edited?

continued

After a draft has been accepted and approved:

10. How will we implement this policy?

    What will the timeline be for implementation?

    What catechesis will be required? Who will be responsible for this?

11. How will we judge the effectiveness of this policy?

    When will we evaluate the policy?

_____

_____

_____

_____

_____

_____

_____

_____

_____

_____

_____

_____

_____

_____

_____

_____

■ Policy-Making Exercise D

Subject: Marriage preparation

Example of pastoral leadership and community responsibility

Introductory statement of policy:

401.1.1 Policy *The parish community shall take responsibility for preparing couples not only for their wedding day but for the lifetime commitment of living a Christian marriage.*

1. Who will be involved in addressing this issue?

2. What is the present parish practice in regard to preparing couples for marriage?

   The above policy clearly indicates that it is the community's responsibility to care for engaged couples. Who else — besides the clergy and pastoral staff — is involved in marriage preparation? Note also that the above policy refers to a lifetime commitment of Christian marriage. What is the parish currently doing for marriage enrichment?

3. Review church documentation or other available resources provided by the diocese.

4. What values are at stake in the above policy?

   Why do you think it was necessary for the diocese to issue a policy like this?

   What values does the committee wish to articulate at this stage?

5. How might the parish take greater responsibility for marriage preparation?

   What are the options, and what ideas can the committee generate?

continued

6. Prioritize the ideas and options.

7. Who else should be consulted in this process? engaged couples? recently married couples? one of the diocesan offices?

8. Would a written policy provide a clear statement of the community's beliefs about and commitment to Christian married life?

   Who will prepare a draft of a policy and of whatever procedures may be necessary?

After a draft has been prepared:

9. Does the draft address all the priorities of the committee?

   Is the proposal clear and feasible?

After a draft has been accepted and approved:

10. How will this policy be implemented?

    Will it need to be implemented in stages?

    How will the community be informed?

    Who will oversee the process?

11. How will we judge the effectiveness of the policy and its procedures?

    When will we evaluate this policy and its procedures?

■ Policy-Making Exercise E

Subject: Access for people with disabilities

Example of pastoral care and the rights of the faithful

Introductory statement of policy:

202.16.1 Policy *Provision shall be made for easy access for the elderly and those with physical disabilities.*

1. Who will be involved in addressing this issue?

   Because it has direct implications for the physical plant of the parish, a facilities committee could be included in the discussion process.

2. What is the physical arrangement for access by people with disabilities?

   Perhaps there is already some access that needs to be improved. Is there space in the assembly for wheelchairs?

3. Review documentation.

   In this case, in addition to church documentation there may be additional documentation from the city or state.

4. What are the values that underlie this policy? For example: inclusiveness, love and respect for others with physical disabilities.

5. What would it take to bring the parish's facilities up to the standard set by this policy? What are the options? What are the obstacles?

continued

6. Prioritize the options.

7. After reviewing the priorities, would further consultation be advisable? For example, would an architect or contractor be able to offer some options?

8. Is a policy required, or would a statement of action be sufficient? A permanent policy may state a commitment of the parish to inclusiveness in a way that an action statement would not. How will we reach a consensus on this issue? Who will prepare a draft?

After a draft has been prepared:

9. Does the proposal resolve the issue?
What is needed to make it more precise?

After a draft has been accepted and approved:

10. How will this draft be implemented?
Who will take responsibility for whatever needs to be done to execute this policy?
Has a timeline been set?

11. How will we judge the success of this policy?

■ Policy-Making Exercise F

Subject: Training catechumenate directors

Example of ministerial expectations and standards

Introductory statement of policy:

102.5.1 Policy *Parish catechumenate directors oversee the organization and pastoral implementation of the order of initiation. They are to be well prepared for their ministry and are to minister in close collaboration with the pastor, pastoral staff, parish pastoral council, parish liturgy committee and director of religious education.*

1. Who will be involved in addressing this issue?

2. Policy 102.5.1 addresses the concern for the preparation of catechumenate ministers, in particular the parish director. This presumes first of all that there is a catechumenate and secondly that someone other than a permanent staff person has been designated the parish catechumenate director. These initial assumptions might need to be addressed before the parish deals directly with this policy.

   Presuming that there is a parish catechumenate with a director, how does our parish ensure that there is adequate training for the director?

   Is there a budget for this purpose? Is this expectation found in the director's job description?

3. Review church documentation.

   A review of the RCIA might be helpful; the committee may need some background information on the order of Christian initiation. There also may be some standards or other polices that the diocese has in place regarding ministerial formation.

continued

4. What values are at stake in the above policy?

   What are some of the parish's values that are in sync with this policy?

5. What recommendations for policy can the committee propose?

   What are some related issues that may be in conflict with some of the committee's recommendations? For example, if a policy is established for training the catechumenate director but there is no policy for any other ministerial positions, will this inconsistency create a conflict? Will a recommended policy on this issue require that another policy be made?

6. Prioritize the options.

7. Is further consultation called for?

8. Is the committee dedicated to drafting a policy and perhaps also some procedures?

   Who will take responsibility for preparing a draft?

After a draft has been prepared:

9. Does the proposed policy adequately address the diocesan policy?

   Does this policy need to be edited?

After a draft has been accepted and approved:

10. How will this policy be implemented? When? Who will be responsible for seeing that it is adhered to?

11. How will we judge the effectiveness of this policy?

    When will we make this evaluation?

    Who will do the evaluating?

■ Policy-Making Exercise G

Subject: Wedding music

Example of vision statement

Introductory statement of policy:

404.15.1 Policy *The selection of music for the wedding liturgy is often a sensitive issue for couples, parish musicians and parish staff. The choice of music at weddings must be in accord with all the norms governing music in liturgy, especially those found in* Liturgical Music Today *and* Music in Catholic Worship.

1. Who will be involved in addressing this issue?

   The subject matter clearly calls for the involvement of the parish musician and those who are responsible for marriage preparation.

2. What is the current parish practice and/or policy regarding music at wedding liturgies?

   What is the experience of those involved in these celebrations?

   Does parish practice meet the expectations of the above policy?

3. Review church documentation.

   In addition to the resources noted in the policy itself, are there other pieces of documentation or commentary that should be reviewed before proceeding further?

continued

4. What values are at stake in the above policy?

   The above policy is more visionary than directive because it is not specific about the kind of music that should be used. Nevertheless, what does the policy seem to expect of parish communities?

   What values might be operative in our parish?

   What are the committee's assumptions about wedding celebrations?

   This is likely to be a sensitive issue with a number of opposing positions. What are the fears that underlie any consideration of a policy on this issue?

5. What are some reasonable options that would flow from the spirit of the diocesan policy?

   What practical steps could be taken to move toward achieving the goals of this policy? What values can the whole committee assent to?

6. Prioritize the options.

7. Is further consultation or study necessary?

8. Is the committee prepared to move toward a written statement of policy?

   Who will prepare a draft? When can the committee expect to see a draft?

After a draft has been prepared:

9. Will the draft meet the community's needs at this stage?

   Does it need to be strengthened, or does it need some built-in flexibility for meeting pastoral circumstances?

continued

After a draft has been accepted and approved:

10. How will this policy be implemented?

    Will it be an interim policy or a permanent policy?

    How will the community, especially engaged couples, be made aware of this policy?

    Will this policy appear in print somewhere?

11. How will this policy be evaluated? Who will do the evaluating? When will this policy be evaluated?

_____

_____

_____

_____

_____

_____

_____

_____

_____

_____

_____

_____

_____

_____

_____

_____

Decision Making and the Process of Drafting Policy: A Few Summary Principles

The preceding discussion of policies and procedures gave some rationale for policy making and provided pastoral advice on how to create and interpret policy. The following summary of pastoral principles can serve as a helpful reminder and guide to those entrusted with decision making.

1. *Approach policy making from a positive frame of mind.*

Ask yourself, "How can we fashion a policy that will help foster a mature sacramental life? What kind of policy do we need to help us better serve the community?" Be clear about the value underlying the need for a policy and a procedure. *Let the positive value of the policy shine through the text.* Be careful not to get trapped into simply reacting to a bad experience. Avoid turning policy making into a corrective action.

2. *Not all issues carry the same weight.*

Design a process commensurate with the degree of the issue's importance. Set limits so that the process doesn't go on endlessly. But in all cases, include some form of consultation.

3. *Use structures that are already in place.*

Depending on the issue under discussion, use structures or systems already in place both for consultation and brainstorming as well as for eventual decision making, when that is appropriate. Look to the parish pastoral council, the liturgy committee, the spiritual life commission, the pastoral staff and whatever other resources are already available. Be sure to provide background information and any necessary catechesis that would be helpful to placing the issue in context.

4. *Let the consultation include in some way those who will be affected by the policies and procedures.*

When a policy will affect a particular group of people — for example, engaged couples — invite some representatives into the discussion. If a policy will affect a large percentage of the parish, a more broad-based consultation may be appropriate. For instance, you might announce an open meeting or publish a draft of the proposed policy in the weekly parish bulletin and invite people to respond. At times a parish survey might be useful, but use this method sparingly. It can be expensive, labor-intensive and difficult to formulate well.

5. *If this is an issue that will affect you directly or if you have very strong feelings about it, invite someone other than yourself to be the facilitator in the consultation and policy-making process.*

When a pastor, for instance, asks someone else to facilitate a consultation and policy-making meeting, he is able to enter into the discussion more freely. If he feels very strongly about an issue, acting as facilitator might only inhibit what otherwise could be a fruitful discussion. Not being the facilitator will also enable the pastor to hear others' views more freely.

6. *Believe that the Holy Spirit can speak through all the faithful.*

No one person has all the answers, and there are many ways of looking at an issue. Every parishioner has a point of view worth listening to. Even in the voice of opposition one can hear concerns and values that are valid. When strong objections are raised or positions are proposed that contradict your beliefs, resist the temptation to correct or rebuke. Listen patiently. Many objections are often tempered by the group process itself.

The facilitator needs to be sensitive to the introverts in the process who may need some quiet time to ponder a proposal. The facilitator may need to ask explicitly for the opinions of those who may be unusually silent.

Allow yourself the freedom to change your own opinion. Don't be stubborn. If someone comes up with a good idea, listen well and change your opinion, if appropriate.

Be careful about making remarks implying that only people with theological degrees or special credentials will understand the issue. If in your heart you approach the process thinking, "These people are ignorant and hopeless," then they will pick up that attitude and it will only lead to resentment and resistance to further recommendations.

Remember that *the ultimate value of formulating policies and procedures is not to produce a paper product but to foster a renewal of sacramental life.* Our hope is that a community will come to appreciate the liturgy and the sacraments more deeply and will integrate the meaning and celebration of these liturgical experiences into their lives individually and as members of the church.

7. *Be optimistic and visionary.*

Give imagination a chance to work. If you respond to an idea by saying, "That will never work; it's unreasonable," then the discussion will end and any further creative ideas might be buried. Being optimistic and visionary also means avoiding placing blame on any one person or group. Most problems are the result of a system that isn't working, not a person or group that isn't working.

Being optimistic also means not taking things personally. When people strongly disagree with your position, don't conclude that it is a referendum against you.

Finally, when the idea or solution you prefer doesn't find a good hearing, let it go and go on to the next issue. Work toward consensus, but don't expect everyone to agree.

8. *Be flexible.*

One of the pitfalls in policy making is creating a policy that leaves no room for flexibility. The ultimate purpose of creating sacramental policies and procedures is to serve the community. Establishing rigid policies that leave no room for exceptions only tends to alienate parishioners and raise the stress levels of the pastoral staff. Issues that arise around weddings and funerals, for example, often require pastoral sensitivity and a good dose of flexibility.

Tension will inevitably arise between good liturgical style and form and the understanding of those for whom the policy was intended. It will not help to establish a good, consistent order in a parish if there are more exceptions to than observances of a policy. Pastoral sensitivity must play a major role in policy making and in the application of policy. With each policy a parish proposes, it must use pastoral sensitivity and flexibility as a checkpoint.

9. *Never introduce and make a decision on an important issue at the same meeting.*

Even if the issue seems simple and obvious at the time, it is better to introduce, discuss and propose at one meeting but then leave the actual decision making for the next meeting.

If new ideas emerge that suggest a significant change in the proposal, don't spend a lot of time in the session doing a committee edit. Get the ideas down and let someone write out the revised proposal and bring it back at a later date. Even as you allow for changes, set time limits on the process. Don't drag the process out hoping that you can arrive at 100% agreement.

The purpose of the meeting should be clear at the start. Is the group gathered for information sharing, consultation, decision making or a combination thereof?

10. *Be clear about how a decision will be made and by whom.*

Implicit in all of these steps is the presumption that everyone is clear on how decision making happens in the parish. If this is not clear, resentment can follow later.

When the pastor exercises the authority to give formal approval to or veto any decision, this should be known up front. It is not an unreasonable use of pastoral authority. The pastor or administrator of a parish should not be placed in the awkward position of unconditionally accepting majority opinion even when in conscience he believes he will not be able to live with the policy. However, if the process of policy making has gone well, the pastor or administrator should not be faced with having to use veto power very often. If the veto is being used frequently, then the process itself may need to be reexamined along with the understanding and exercise of one's authority. It is also possible that there exist some deeply rooted conflicting theologies of church and sacrament that need to be looked at squarely.

11. *Communicate and publicize the policy.*

There's not much point in creating policies and procedures if the community isn't aware of them. Create a system or plan by which the policies and procedures are announced and made available. Date each policy. Begin a parish policy binder in which all policies can be found. This will give new staff members an opportunity to learn quickly the operative policies and procedures of the parish. In implementing policies and procedures, the question of accountability also needs to be addressed. Who will hold us accountable for the observance of the policies and procedures?

12. *Plan to review policies and procedures at regular intervals.*

Few policies and procedures are written with a 100-year guarantee. Once approved and implemented, the shortcomings of a policy or procedure may soon become evident. As circumstances change, the policies and procedures need to reflect the changing life of the community and the evolving sacramental discipline of the universal church. Be patient. Sometimes it takes a long time to get it right. Without making a big fuss about it, take time to review policies and procedures and to make whatever adjustments may be necessary to serve the community better.

POLICIES AND PROCEDURES

OF THE

ARCHDIOCESE OF CHICAGO

■

Book IV

The Sanctifying Office of the Church

§100

THE SACRAMENTS OF INITIATION

■

contents

§100

THE SACRAMENTS OF INITIATION

Introduction: A Vision for Sacramental Life

There is no greater joy for a parish community than to experience the initiation of new members at the Easter Vigil. On this night, "most blessed of all nights, chosen by God to see Christ rising from the dead" (from the *Exultet*), the community encounters the risen Christ in the initiation of new members; they hear the Easter Gospel proclaimed anew as they see men and women rise with Christ to a new life of grace.

The font of baptism is like a tomb; in these waters Christians imitate the death of Christ as they leave behind their old selves. The font of baptism is like a womb; here new Christians, freed from the power of darkness, are chosen by God as sons and daughters who claim eternal life as their promised inheritance. This sacramental sharing in Christ's dying and rising becomes the pattern for the Christian's life (*Catechism of the Catholic Church*, #1212–1419).

Before the community calls catechumens and candidates to the sacraments of initiation, it must do all that it can to foster a genuine conversion in those to be initiated. What is seen and experienced in the sacraments of initiation ought to be a reflection of a genuine conversion of mind and heart in response to the challenging word of God. It may require a radical refashioning of one's life, thinking, values and commitment.

The process of conversion is lifelong and is uniquely connected to different levels of human development. Christian initiation presumes that the word of God has already begun to transform the life of the individual, that there has been a spirit of cooperation on the part of the person to put into practice what one believes and the desire to pattern one's life on the teaching of Christ.

When celebrating infant baptism, the church looks to the parents whose home must become the place where faith and conversion will be nurtured in the child. While the initiation of infants may be celebrated at different times during the year, the celebration always reflects the spirit of the Easter Mystery.

The *Rite of Baptism for Children* is used exclusively for the initiation of infants. At the same time, the church's theology and pastoral care of infants and their parents is influenced by the *Rite of Christian Initiation of Adults*. For that reason and to support a pastoral and theological synthesis, this document will treat infant baptism and adult initiation side by side.

The whole Christian community is called to take responsibility for preparing men, women, and children for the sacraments of initiation. As the introduction to the *Rite of Christian Initiation of Adults* states:

> The people of God, as represented by the local church, should understand and show by their concern that the initiation of adults is the responsibility of all the baptized. Therefore, the community must always be fully prepared in the pursuit of its apostolic vocation to give help to those who are searching for Christ. In the various circumstances of daily life, even as in the apostolate, all the followers of Christ have the obligation of spreading the faith according to their abilities. (RCIA, #9)

As the introduction to the *Rite of Baptism for Children* states: "Before and after the celebration of the sacrament, the child has a right to the love and help of the community" (*Rite of Baptism for Children*, #4).

By actively participating in the formation and initiation of new members, the faithful themselves are gradually renewed in their own baptismal vocation. The deeper their own conversion, the more effective they will be in leading others to mature faith.

Conversion of mind and heart, a sufficient acquaintance with Christian teaching, as well as a spirit of faith and charity (RCIA, #120), obviously take time to achieve. The formation envisioned in the order of initiation must be spread over a time frame that allows for a consistent hearing and reflection on the word of God, spiritual counsel or direction, a thorough catechesis, learning to pray with the church, sharing in the church's apostolic work and through association with the faithful learning from them the values, morals and spirit of the Catholic community.

While the process of Christian initiation as outlined in the *Rite of Christian Initiation of Adults* may at first appear to be difficult to implement, its vision for fostering a mature Christian life is essential to every parish's well-being. In other words, the paradigm of formation for ministering to new members becomes the model for the parish's life and mission.

All Christians are called to an ongoing conversion, to a more intimate participation in the death and resurrection of Christ, to a fuller appreciation of the Christian tradition of prayer, creed, an ongoing faith formation and a more active role in the church's mission. Consequently, all pastoral efforts to fully implement the order of Christian initiation will inevitably affect the life of the parish.

The implementation of this sacramental vision may point out inconsistencies in parish priorities or ways of doing things that need to be reevaluated. This understandably does not happen overnight. But parish renewal demands that we earnestly review our priorities and our parish structures and systems in order to refashion the parish for more effective service in the future.

The process of Christian initiation then is not just one more thing a parish is expected to provide. It lies at the heart of its vocation. The ministry of evangelization and initiation influences every area of parish life and indeed provides a theological and sacramental vision that holds all the rest together.

The pastoral challenge is to review how consistent our overall sacramental and catechetical parochial practice is with the theological and sacramental principles encapsulated in the *Rite of Christian Initiation of Adults* and the *Rite of Baptism for Children*. These documents provide a picture of what it means to be church. This does not imply that we can do without religious education programs and Catholic schools, but rather that these institutions can receive direction from the vision found in these documents.

What follows here is intended to assist parish communities in the full implementation of the *Rite of Christian Initiation of Adults* and the *Rite of Baptism for Children*. The initiation of new members is a ministry to persons which presumes a pastoral sensitivity and respect for the unique background and personal history of individuals. It is difficult to provide absolute norms or preset programs that will apply in every situation. Initiation is a process that demands flexibility on the part of all and a humility that enables us to see the Holy Spirit working in our midst.

These policies and procedures are also intended to respect the cultural diversity in the archdiocese, which must naturally be considered in establishing parish practice. Parishes that share common cultural experiences are encouraged to reflect upon the implications of specific cultural values and customs and collaboratively move toward a consistent practice.

While respecting the need for pastoral adaptation, there are nevertheless pastoral norms that need to be honored. These policies and procedures attempt to enumerate a number of these and to clarify what questions have already surfaced from pastoral practice. These policies and procedures are not exhaustive, nor do they dispense of the need to carefully study the *Rite of Christian Initiation of Adults,* the *Rite of Baptism for Children* and other relevant church documents.

The Archdiocesan Christian Initiation Board, consisting of several archdiocesan agencies in a collaborative style of ministry, exists to serve parish communities in the ongoing implementation of the *Rite of Christian Initiation of Adults,* the *Rite of Baptism for Children* and these policies and procedures. It is committed to the development of the vision and direction which these documents represent.

What is provided here is intended to highlight some key areas of concern for our local church. In promoting a consistent practice in regard to the sacraments of initiation, the hope is that the vision behind these rites will be strengthened. Through mutual support and accountability it is hoped that all parishes will find it easier to implement and sustain a common vision.

§101

Preparation for the Sacraments of Initiation

§101.1 Ministry to Adults

101.1.1 Policy *The* Rite of Christian Initiation of Adults *is normative in the archdiocese of Chicago. Every parish shall be prepared to minister to those who seek Christ and initiation into the church through the implementation of the current order of initiation mandated for the universal church.*

Procedures

a) The parish pastoral council, which shares the pastoral concern for the life of the entire parish, should make every effort to see that the *Rite of Christian Initiation of Adults* becomes a consistent and well integrated part of the life of the parish.

b) The parish should provide complete and thorough formation for catechumens (unbaptized persons). This includes evangelization that can lead to genuine conversion, a suitable catechesis accommodated to adults and the liturgical year, familiarity with the Christian way of life, the celebration of rites, the opportunity for spiritual counsel or direction, formation in private prayer and public worship and the opportunity to "learn how to work actively with others to spread the Gospel and build up the church" (RCIA, #75 and archdiocesan Religious Education Policies).

c) When a parish's resources do not permit them to maintain their own catechumenal process, the parish may collaborate with another parish or other parishes to provide one well-developed process of initiation for the area. This is especially helpful either when first implementing the *Rite of Christian Initiation of Adults* or in smaller parishes or when language, cultural or disability needs dictate. In these cases, the rites are still ordinarily celebrated in the catechumen's parish (National Statutes, #4).

101.1.2 Policy *The term "catechumen" is only to be used for the unbaptized who have been admitted into the order of catechumens. Baptized Christians being received into the full communion of the Roman Catholic Church are referred to as "candidates" (National Statutes, #2).*

101.1.3 Policy *The integrity of the church's rites is to be maintained. When extraordinary circumstances prevent the catechumen from completing all the steps of the catechumenate, when the catechumen has reached a depth of Christian conversion and a degree of religious maturity, or when it is a question of disability, advanced age or serious illness (RCIA, #381 – 389), the parish may receive the archbishop's permission to use the abbreviated form of the order of initiation as given in the* Rite of Christian Initiation of Adults, Part II, *#2, by contacting the Office for Divine Worship or the Office of the Chancellor.*

101.1.4 Policy *The following persons may be invited to participate in the catechumenal process with the unbaptized to whatever extent may be helpful to their spiritual formation:*

1) candidates who were baptized as Roman Catholics but are uncatechized and now wish to complete their initiation through confirmation and eucharist;

2) adults who were baptized in non-Catholic Christian denominations and are preparing to be received into the full communion of the Roman Catholic Church.

Procedures

a) The scope of formation necessary for the baptized candidates will depend upon their background and need. Part II, #4 and #5 of the *Rite of Christian Initiation of Adults* should be studied carefully to see how best to provide for the needs of these candidates.

b) In ministering to baptized candidates, extremes should be avoided. We ought not presume someone baptized as an infant possesses a mature faith and fully comprehends the meaning and responsibilities of the Christian life. However, candidates who have had a solid Christian upbringing and who give evidence of mature faith and Christian practice should not be expected to follow the same formation process as those who are first coming to faith.

c) A clear distinction must always be made between those who are unbaptized and those who are already baptized but completing their initiation through the sacraments of confirmation and eucharist or being received into the full communion of the Roman Catholic Church. This is important so that the unique and irrevocable gift of baptism is respected and its significance in no way overlooked (National Statutes, #30).

§101.2 Ministry to Children of Catechetical Age

101.2.1 Policy *The formation of children of catechetical age, including adolescents, shall follow the general pattern of the catechumenate as far as possible. Part II, #1 of the* Rite of Christian Initiation of Adults *pertains specifically to children of catechetical age (canon 852.1 and National Statutes, #18).*

Procedures

a) Pastors are reminded that once a child has reached catechetical age (approximately seven years old), the *Rite of Baptism for Children* is no longer the proper ritual to use. Unbaptized children of catechetical age should be welcomed into a children's catechumenate (RCIA, #252–330), which takes the children's age and background into account. The approval and cooperation of the parents or legal guardians should always be sought.

b) The *Rite of Christian Initiation of Adults* provides a theological, liturgical and pastoral framework for ministry to children preparing for the initiation sacraments. It presumes that the children will be joined by their peers who can support them in their journey of faith (RCIA, #254).

c) The initiation of children must be understood within the larger picture of the parish community. The parish staff and pastoral council will want to work closely with parents to provide a healthy and effective environment within which young children can grow in age, wisdom, and grace. Parish efforts in religious education, youth and family ministry and liturgy need to be coordinated in order to provide a consistent and well-integrated vision and pastoral approach.

d) The Offices for Divine Worship, Evangelization, Catholic Education, Religious Education and Special Religious Development (SPRED) can assist parishes who are developing suitable programs to meet local pastoral needs in ministering to children.

101.2.2 Policy *The permission of at least one parent (legal guardian) is required before a child is accepted into the catechumenate and before the child is initiated into the church. Parents are encouraged to participate in the process of formation to whatever extent they are able and to offer the support and example the children need (RCIA, #254). In the absence of parental support, sponsors are to be chosen to take the place of the parents, (RCIA, #260).*

101.2.3 Policy *The needs of children preparing for reception into the full communion of the Roman Catholic Church may be similar to children who are catechumens. Consequently, their formation and preparation for confirmation and eucharist may be accomplished together with children who are catechumens.*

Ministry to Infants and Their Parents   §101.3

101.3.1 Policy *Catholic parents preparing for the baptism of their infant are expected to participate in a process of sacramental preparation before the baptism of their child. Godparents may also be encouraged to participate.*

101.3.2 Policy *Every parish or group of parishes shall ensure sacramental preparation for parents prior to the baptism of their first child. Appropriate catechesis for parents with additional children should also be offered.*

Procedures

a) Baptismal preparation of parents may take a variety of forms, but it should include some of the faithful and never be considered only the priest's or deacon's responsibility.

   Some form of adaptation may be necessary for parents participating in a preparation program who have already participated in a baptismal preparation program for their first child.

b) This ministry to parents should be viewed as spiritual guidance or formation and pastoral care as well as catechesis. The preparation of parents for their child's baptism should be characterized by a sincere love and concern for the family, a desire to deepen their relationship to the church and assist them in arriving at a deeper appreciation of baptism and their own vocation as Christian parents.

   In the case where parents have not been fully initiated in the celebration of baptism, confirmation, and first eucharist, a ministry to parents may be an opportunity to encourage the parents to complete their initiation.

   What we expect for adults and children of catechetical age through the order of initiation we hope to see begun and developed at home as parents provide an environment and the personal example that will foster and nurture the child's faith (*Catechism of the Catholic Church*, #1250–1255).

c) A request for infant baptism cannot ordinarily be refused. However, a baptism can be delayed until such time as the parents or at least one of the parents are ready and able to assume the responsibility entrusted to Christian parents in the rite. This occasion should be viewed as an opportunity for evangelization, not placing an undue burden on the parents but helping them to grow in the spiritual life from whatever level of faith they may be.

§102

Ministers of Initiation

The Christian initiation of adults, children and infants takes place in the midst of the community. Pastors need to remind the faithful again and again of their spiritual kinship with those who are to be initiated. They should be encouraged to support and pray for catechumens and candidates, infants and their parents.

By living lives of charity and justice and by taking an active part in the mission of the church and its worship, members of the faithful give a convincing witness to all who are preparing for Christian initiation or growing up Christian.

In reaching out to catechumens and candidates, members of the faithful may be selected as sponsors or spiritual guides or chosen to introduce the catechumens and candidates to the various apostolates of the church through a period of apostolic apprenticeship.

Collaboration   §102.1

102.1.1 Policy *Because the initiation of adults is "the responsibility of all the baptized" (RCIA, #9), pastors shall associate with themselves men and women of the parish who, as catechists, sponsors, and in other roles, collaborate with them in the formation and initiation of new members. It is the pastor's responsibility to see that those who assist in the initiation process have been properly trained.*

§102.2 Catechists

102.2.1 Policy *Catechists who minister to adults and children shall be well trained in the role of presiding at prayer and in catechetical methodology according to* Sharing the Light of Faith *and* Adult Catechesis in the Christian Community. *Their instruction should be filled with the spirit of the Gospel, adapted to the liturgical signs and cycle of the church year, suited to the needs of catechumens and candidates, and, as far as possible, enriched by local traditions.*

102.2.2 Policy *Catechists who are properly deputed by their pastors may preside at the minor exorcisms and blessings (RCIA, #12, 16, 34.5, 91, 96; Book of Blessings #519 – 521) and at celebrations of the Word of God (RCIA, #81 – 89).*

§102.3 Sponsors and Godparents

102.3.1 Policy *Catechumens and candidates need the support and spiritual companionship of a sponsor during their formation. This role is ordinarily filled by a parish sponsor who may be chosen later as the godparent for the sacraments of initiation (RCIA, #10).*

102.3.2 Policy *At the time of election, the catechumen, in consultation with the parish priest and the initiation team, chooses a godparent in accord with the ritual norms of the order of initiation. The godparent can be the catechumen's spouse (RCIA, #11, 123, 404).*

102.3.3 Policy *At the beginning of Lent the candidate chooses a sponsor for the celebration of confirmation in keeping with the general norms of the church. The confirmation sponsor can be the candidate's spouse, but cannot be the candidate's parent (canons 892 and 893).*

102.3.4 Policy *In the baptism of infants parents take responsibility for choosing a godparent or godparents who will serve as good examples for living the Catholic way of life. A godparent can later serve as the sponsor of the child when he/she is confirmed.*

102.3.5 Policy *Although the selection of two godparents is customary, only one godparent is required for baptism. A godparent can be either male or female. If two godparents are chosen, one must be male and one female (canon 873). A godparent must also be a fully initiated Roman Catholic who is free to celebrate the sacraments (canons 892 and 893). A baptized, non-Catholic Christian can be chosen as a Christian witness provided there is at least one Catholic godparent (canon 874.2).*

102.3.6 Policy *A godparent must have completed his or her sixteenth year unless, for just cause, the pastor or minister of the sacrament makes an exception. Each godparent must be a confirmed Catholic who has also received first communion and is leading a life in harmony with the Catholic faith and the role of a sponsor. A godparent cannot be a parent of the one to be baptized and/or confirmed and cannot be bound by any canonical penalty.*

In addition to the explicit canonical requirements (canon 874), sponsors and godparents should be ready to commit the time and personal care necessary to nurture and support the candidate, whether a child or an adult. Ideally, they should be willing and available to participate in the catechumenate with their candidate or in the special preparations designed for the parents and family of an infant. One's godparents can never be changed, since they were the historical witnesses to the baptism and entered a permanent spiritual relationship with the baptized.

§102.4   Pastors

102.4.1 Policy *Pastors and associate pastors have a special responsibility to oversee the rites of Christian initiation, to preside and preach at them, and to prepare the faithful by an appropriate catechesis.*

102.4.2 Policy *Pastors and associate pastors in the archdiocese of Chicago have the authority to depute properly prepared catechists to preside at the minor exorcisms and blessings (RCIA, #12, 16, 34.5, 91, 96; Book of Blessings, #519–521) and at celebrations of the Word of God (RCIA #81–89; and* Responses to Frequently Asked Questions on the Christian Initiation of Adults for the Province of Chicago, #20).

Catechumenate Directors §102.5

102.5.1 Policy *Parish catechumenate directors oversee the organization and pastoral implementation of the order of initiation. They are to be well prepared for their ministry and are to minister in close collaboration with the pastor, pastoral staff, parish pastoral council, parish liturgy committee and director of religious education.*

Special Note: *A parish minister other than the catechumenate director may be delegated to oversee the pastoral care of parents preparing for the baptism of their children. This person should be encouraged to collaborate with the catechumenate director to ensure that the parish develops a consistent pastoral vision for Christian initiation.*

Bishops, Priests and Deacons §102.6

102.6.1 Policy *The ordinary ministers of baptism are bishops, priests, and deacons. In imminent danger of death, when no priest or deacon is available, any member of the faithful, indeed anyone with the right intention, may and sometimes must administer baptism (Christian Initiation, General Introduction, #11, 16).*

102.6.2 Policy *Any bishop or priest who baptizes an adult or a child of catechetical age should also confer confirmation. The celebration of confirmation and reception of eucharist should not be deferred (RCIA, #14, canon 885.2; see Faculties 802.1).*

102.6.3 Policy *When a priest receives a Christian into full communion with the Catholic church, he receives from the law itself (canon 883.2) the faculty to confirm the candidate for reception and is obliged to use it for the sake of the candidate (canon 885.2). The confirmation of such candidates for reception should not be deferred, nor should they be admitted to the eucharist until they are confirmed (National Statutes, #35; see Faculties 802.1).*

102.6.4 Policy *Priests who do not have archdiocesan faculties require a mandate from the Office of the Chancellor if they are to baptize an adult. Thereafter, no additional mandate or authorization to confirm is required as such priests possess this faculty from the law, as do priests who baptize adults in the exercise of their pastoral office (National Statutes, #12).*

102.6.5 Policy *According to the norms issued by the Holy See, a priest must obtain special delegation in order to validly confirm a baptized Catholic, even if the candidate was uncatechized and participated in the catechumenate. In the archdiocese of Chicago, this is obtained from the Office of the Chancellor or the director of the Office for Divine Worship. (See Faculties 802.1)*

§103

Celebrating the Rites

One of the most important components of the order of initiation is the careful preparation and celebration of the various rites that mark the progress of catechumens and candidates in their journey to initiation. The full impact of the experience of initiation cannot be felt without these necessary ritual moments being given the proper attention that they deserve.

Rites for Catechumens Integral   §103.1

103.1.1 Policy *The major rites provided for catechumens cannot be omitted because the liturgies of the* Rite of Christian Initiation of Adults *are integral to the whole initiation process. They should be well prepared so that they will inspire the faithful and effectively touch the lives of the catechumens.*

Optional Rites for Baptized but Uncatechized Adults   §103.2

103.2.1 Policy *Pastoral staffs are encouraged to use the optional rites for baptized but uncatechized adults as found in the* Rite of Christian Initiation of Adults, *Part II, #4. These can be celebrated along with the rites for the unbaptized as provided in the appendix to the RCIA, Additional Combined Rites (RCIA, #505 – 594).*

> **Special Note:** *Although the* Rite of Baptism for Children *does not provide preparatory rites, parish ministers should be encouraged to pray with the parents and to make use of the rites provided in the* Book of Blessings, *e.g.,* Orders for the Blessing of a Mother Before Childbirth and After Childbirth, *and the* Order for the Blessing of a Child Not Yet Baptized (#236 – 278, 156 – 173).

§103.3   Celebrating the Appropriate Rites

103.3.1 Policy *The Rite of Acceptance into the Order of Catechumens (RCIA, #41–74, 260–276) is celebrated with unbaptized candidates.*

The Rite of Welcoming the Candidates (RCIA, #411–433) is celebrated with baptized but previously uncatechized adults or children of catechetical age who are seeking to complete their Christian initiation through the sacraments of confirmation and eucharist or to be received into the full communion of the Catholic church.

When unbaptized children have received a preliminary catechetical formation and have shown signs of initial faith and conversion appropriate to their age, they are to celebrate the Rite of Acceptance into the Order of Catechumens (RCIA, #260–276).

Procedures

a) The Rite of Acceptance into the Order of Catechumens and the Rite of Welcoming the Candidates are celebrated in the parish church at a time when a good number of the parishioners can participate.

b) The names of those accepted into the Order of Catechumens should be recorded in a parish register of catechumens (RCIA, #46).

c) Once accepted as catechumens, these men and women are considered part of the household of Christ. Consequently, they are entitled to celebrate their marriage in the Catholic church. One who dies as a catechumen receives a Christian burial (RCIA, #47).

d) Children, who are catechumens or candidates, may participate in the Rite of Acceptance into the Order of Catechumens or the Rite of Welcoming Candidates along with their parents who are celebrating these rites (RCIA, #505–529).

e) In the case of children, the celebration of the Rite of Acceptance into the Order of Catechumens or of Welcoming the Candidates may take place in a community of the children's peers.

Combined Rite of Election and Call to Continuing Conversion

§103.4

103.4.1 Policy *In the archdiocese of Chicago, the combined Rite of Election and the Call to Continuing Conversion is celebrated annually with a bishop at the Cathedral at the beginning of Lent.*

Procedures

All parishes receive an annual invitation to participate in the Rite of Election and the Call to Continuing Conversion at the cathedral. The names of the catechumens and candidates are sent to the Office for Divine Worship by the parish. Catechumens who will be baptized at the next Easter Vigil celebration are expected to participate in the archdiocesan celebration of the Rite of Election and the Call to Continuing Conversion. Candidates (baptized Christians) are encouraged to participate but are not obliged to do so.

Celebration of the Rite of Election at the Parish

§103.5

103.5.1 Policy *When for pastoral reasons it is not possible for one or several catechumens to attend the archdiocesan celebration of the Rite of Election, delegation for a pastor to celebrate the rite in a catechumen's parish may be obtained from the Office for Divine Worship or the Office of the Chancellor.*

Procedures

a) A record of the catechumens' election should be kept at the parish, listing their name, their godparent's name, the presider and the date of the celebration. This record is kept at the parish of the elect.

b) The names of those who participated in the Calling of Candidates to Continuing Conversion may also be recorded in the parish record book, clearly indicating their status as baptized candidates.

c) The Rite of Calling Candidates to Continuing Conversion is optional. It may be celebrated at the cathedral or in the parish. No delegation is necessary for the parish priest to preside at this rite.

§103.6 Rite of Election for Children

103.6.1 Policy *The Rite of Election for Children (RCIA, #277 – 290), an optional rite, would ordinarily be celebrated in a separate celebration among the children's peers or at a parish community celebration at the beginning of Lent.*

Procedures

a) Pastors do not need to obtain delegation to celebrate the Rite of Election for Children in the parish.

b) Children who are catechumens may accompany their parents who are also catechumens in the cathedral celebration of the Rite of Election.

§103.7 Lenten Scrutinies

103.7.1 Policy *All three Lenten scrutinies are to be used for the unbaptized catechumens.*

Procedures

a) In celebrating the Lenten scrutinies, the Cycle A readings of the Lectionary may be used during cycles B and C.

b) If for some reason one or more of the major scrutinies and exorcisms could not be celebrated at the appropriate Lenten Sunday Mass, it may be celebrated during the week at a Mass or, if necessary, a Liturgy of the Word.

c) The penitential rites (scrutinies) provided for children of catechetical age (RCIA, #291 – 302) are to be celebrated during the final preparation of the children for baptism.

Reception of Sacraments at One Celebration and in Proper Order

§103.8

103.8.1 Policy *The Christian initiation of adults and children of catechetical age includes at one celebration: baptism, confirmation and the first sharing in eucharist. In accord with the ancient practice of the church, these sacraments are to be received together and in their proper order (RCIA, #215, canon 866, Policy 103.12).*

Procedures

The newly baptized may receive a baptismal garment immediately after their baptism. The use of a stole, the symbol of an ordained minister, is not appropriate.

Site for Baptisms

§103.9

103.9.1 Policy *The celebration of baptism is to take place in the parish church. Baptisms in private homes are not permitted except in cases of emergency. Anyone who baptizes in a case of emergency is obliged to notify the baptized's pastor so that the baptism is recorded in the appropriate register. (See §900, Sacramental Records, Policy 902.2.1.)*

Infants who were baptized in an emergency situation may be brought to the church at a later time to complete the baptismal ceremony, but omitting the pouring of the water. (See Chapter 6, "The Rite of Bringing a Baptized Child to the Church," in the Rite of Baptism for Children.)

§103.10 Baptism by Immersion and Partial Immersion

103.10.1 Policy *"Baptism by immersion is the fuller and more expressive sign of the sacrament and, therefore, provision should be made for its more frequent use in the baptism of adults. The provision of the* Rite of Christian Initiation of Adults *for partial immersion, namely, immersion of the candidate's head, should be taken into account"* (National Statutes, #17).

103.10.2 Policy *In the archdiocese of Chicago, whenever a new church is erected, provision must be made for a font that allows for immersion. When a church is renovated, the font should be constructed to allow for the immersion of infants at least, and for the immersion of adults, if possible. (See* Environment and Art in Catholic Worship, *#76;* Rite of Baptism for Children, *#19, 22;* RCIA *#213;* Catechism of the Catholic Church, *#1214, 1239, 1262, 628.)*

Procedures

In the building of a new church or the renovation of an existing church, the parish should consult with the Archdiocesan Building and Renovation Commission of the Office for Divine Worship regarding the construction of the font.

Confirmation of Adults §103.11

103.11.1 Policy *Baptized and catechized Roman Catholics who, for whatever reason, have not had the opportunity to be confirmed, shall be invited to complete their initiation after an appropriate catechesis. These adults may be confirmed either at the next visit of the bishop to the parish for confirmation, at deanery or vicariate confirmations designed specifically for these adults, or at the Easter Vigil by the priest who has received the necessary delegation to confirm from the Chancellor or the Director of the Office for Divine Worship (see Faculty 802.1.c).*

Confirmation of Children of Catechetical Age §103.12

103.12.1 Policy *All children of catechetical age are to be confirmed and receive the eucharist at the time of their baptism (National Statutes #14,18,19). The integrity and unity of the sacraments of initiation are maintained by not delaying the reception of confirmation or eucharist (RCIA, #215; see canon 883,2° and Faculties 802.1).*

Procedures

a) Pastors should see to it that the above policy is carefully explained to parents and their children who have been baptized in infancy and are following the customary course of delaying confirmation until a later date. Care should be taken to avoid confusion in the community regarding readiness to receive the sacrament of confirmation.

b) The resources of the Catholic school, religious education program, specialized catechesis and youth ministry should be drawn upon in preparing children for Christian initiation. Their sacramental preparation should be distinct from and complementary to their course of study in the Catholic school, religious education program and youth ministry. However, children and adolescents with special needs are more fruitfully catechized after the sacraments of initiation (canon 777).

c) After children are fully initiated, their Christian formation should be continued.

d) At the time when their peers are confirmed, they should be asked to renew their baptismal promises with their peers. When the bishop is present, he may greet them in a special way.

§103.13 Reception into the Full Communion of the Catholic Church

103.13.1 Policy *Adults and children of catechetical age who were baptized in a non-Catholic Christian denomination are formally received into the church through the Rite of Reception of Baptized Christians into the Full Communion of the Catholic Church (RCIA, Part II, #5).*

Procedures

a) Children of parents being received into the full communion of the Catholic church are ordinarily received into the church with their parents.

b) The reception of children and adults into full communion needs to be recorded both in the baptismal and the confirmation registers. Baptized children younger than the catechetical age do not go through any ceremony to be received into the Catholic church. They become members of the church at the same time their parents do (see §902.2.3).

c) The child's original baptism is recorded in the parish baptismal register with a note of their being joined to the Catholic church through the act of their parents' initiation.

103.13.2 Policy *Candidates, including children of catechetical age, who are received into the full communion of the Roman Catholic Church are to be confirmed at the same celebration at which they make their profession of faith and partake of the eucharist. Their confirmation is not to be deferred (National Statutes, #35).*

Age of Confirmation   §103.14

103.14.1 Policy *In the archdiocese of Chicago, children baptized in infancy as Roman Catholics are ordinarily confirmed at the age determined by the NCCB (canon 891).*

Special Note: Catechists and other pastoral ministers should be cautious about attaching an exaggerated expectation of Christian maturity on youth in order to receive the sacrament of confirmation. Care should also be taken not to impose so many requirements for confirmation that confirmation appears to be a reward or graduation. Confirmation is not something that someone achieves or earns, but rather is a gift of God, as are all the sacraments. More emphasis should be placed on the eucharist as the repeatable sacrament of initiation.

Because a move to a younger age (i.e., before first communion) requires special pastoral planning, the Offices for Divine Worship, Religious Education and Catholic Education should be consulted in the development of such a parish plan or policy.

A person with a developmental disability who has been baptized cannot be denied confirmation as long as he/she desires to belong to the community of faith.

The celebration of the sacrament of confirmation for an adult who has mental retardation should be age appropriate, i.e., the person should not be made to feel awkward by being placed at the end of the celebration planned for children.

In some cases it may be appropriate for the parish priest to seek delegation to confirm individuals with disabilities during the Easter season. When the developmentally disabled person is known by the parish priest, the individual is apt to be more comfortable and secure, thus ensuring a more fruitful and dignified celebration.

§104

The Reception of First Communion

One of the goals in restoring the original order of the sacraments of initiation (baptism followed by confirmation followed by first communion) is to foster a greater appreciation for the eucharist as a sacrament of initiation. Each time we share in the eucharist, we are initiated more deeply into the saving death and resurrection of the Lord. Our participation in the eucharist renews our commitment as baptized Christians to carry on Christ's ministry in the world.

The understanding of eucharist as an initiatory sacrament should be carefully taught.

§104.1 Preparation for Eucharist an Integral Part of Catechumenate Process

104.1.1 Policy *The preparation of adults for reception of first eucharist is an integral part of the catechumenate process and should strive to fulfill the goals of a contemporary catechesis for the eucharist outlined in the* National Catechetical Directory *(see* Sharing the Light of Faith, *#121 – 122).*

Concentrated Preparation for Each Sacrament §104.2

104.2.1 Policy *"Catechesis for First Communion is conducted separately from introductory catechesis for the sacrament of penance, since each sacrament deserves its own concentrated preparation. Continued catechesis is given yearly in all catechetical programs for children, inasmuch as the sacraments require lifelong participation and study"* (Sharing the Light of Faith: National Catechetical Directory for Catholics of the United States, #122; see also §107, "The Sacrament of Penance and Christian Initiation," herein).

Special Note: *In preparing children for their first reception of eucharist, parish communities should remember that the reception of eucharist is a sacrament of initiation. Even if the traditional order (baptism, confirmation, eucharist) is not followed when children are confirmed after first eucharist, the celebration of first communion should retain the spirit and meaning of Christian initiation. (See* Sharing the Light of Faith, *#122.)*

Readiness of Candidates §104.3

104.3.1 Policy *Pastors, in consultation with parents, the director of the parish catechumenate, catechists, and other appropriate ministers, are to determine the readiness of the candidates to receive their first communion in keeping with the goals of the* Rite of Christian Initiation of Adults *and the norms of the* National Catechetical Directory. *This readiness must include a sufficient familiarity with the nature of the eucharist in order for the candidate to participate actively and with awareness.*

Procedures

A person with developmental disabilities within a small community of faith can indicate readiness for first communion by the following: relationships with people who share faith and prayer, a sense of the sacred as manifested in behavior, and desire for communion. If those with disabilities cannot use words to express their understanding of communion, they can show their awareness by their manner, the expression in their eyes, their gestures, and the quality of their silence (from *Access to the Sacraments of Initiation*, p. 9).

§105

Times and Schedules

The rites of Christian initiation reach their climax in the celebration of the Easter Vigil. The sacraments of initiation draw their fullest meaning and significance from the solemn celebration of Christ's victory over sin and death. "Those who are baptized are united to Christ in a death like his; buried with him in death, they are given new life again with him, and with him they rise again. For baptism recalls and makes present the paschal mystery itself, because in baptism we pass from the death of sin into life" (*Christian Initiation*, General Introduction, #6).

The entire initiation process and our celebration of the sacraments of baptism, confirmation, and eucharist must respect the integrity of the liturgical year, looking toward the Triduum as the source and climax of the initiation process.

Rite of Acceptance   §105.1

105.1.1 Policy *The Rite of Acceptance into the Order of Catechumens may be celebrated whenever there are unbaptized inquirers who are ready to take this step. This rite may be celebrated a number of times throughout the year, according to pastoral need.*

§105.2   Celebration of the Sacraments of Initiation

105.2.1 Policy *The usual time for the celebration of the sacraments of initiation is the Easter Vigil. The recommendations of the documents regarding initiation outside the usual times should be followed. Even when Christian initiation is celebrated outside the usual times indicated in the* Rite of Christian Initiation of Adults, *the texts for the Sunday Masses of the Easter Season, including the readings from year A, may be used (RCIA, #247).*

§105.3   Infant Baptism

105.3.1 Policy *The celebration of infant baptism should ordinarily take place on Sunday.*

Procedures

a) Infant baptisms are ordinarily celebrated once on a particular Sunday, while honoring ethnic traditions for alternative days for celebrating baptism. The fullest expression of baptism as incorporation into the church is best achieved through a communal celebration that includes all who are to be baptized at one ceremony with members of the faithful participating.

b) Infant baptisms may be celebrated at a regularly scheduled Sunday Mass on a schedule accepted by the pastor in consultation with the parish pastoral council and the liturgy committee. The frequency of celebration at Sunday Mass must take into account the sensitivities of the members of the community. Appropriate days on the liturgical calendar or in the life of the parish should be chosen.

c) Parishes need not schedule the baptism of infants every Sunday. The number of baptisms in the parish and the limitations of space and staff should determine parish scheduling policy.

d) Unless there is a genuine pastoral need, baptisms should not be scheduled during Lent, lest the approaching celebration of Easter with its strong baptismal focus be diminished.

e) The baptismal liturgy should be celebrated according to all the appropriate norms for worship, i.e., participation of the assembly, inclusion of lay ministries, music, etc.

f) It may be more pastorally suitable to celebrate infant baptism at an Easter Sunday Mass when adults are baptized at the Easter Vigil, unless the infants are the children of the adult candidates.

Postbaptismal Catechesis or Mystagogy   §105.4

105.4.1 Policy *A suitable period of mystagogy or postbaptismal catechesis needs to be offered the newly baptized so that they might live more deeply the mysteries they have celebrated. Ordinarily, postbaptismal catechesis and pastoral care should extend for one year (See National Statutes, #24).*

Procedures

a) Each year the newly baptized are invited to celebrate a special Mass of Thanksgiving with the archbishop during the Easter season.

b) Pastoral care of the newly baptized beyond the time of initiation is strongly encouraged. During this period of mystagogy, transition should be made to active sharing in the mission of the church. Of course, the need for ongoing catechesis is presumed.

§106

Special Pastoral Considerations

There are a number of pastoral issues that continue to arise in Christian initiation. The following policies and procedures are intended to assist pastoral ministers in resolving some of the most common issues.

§106.1 Christian Marriages Involving Catechumens

106.1.1 Policy Because catechumens are already joined to the church as part of the household of Christ, they are entitled to celebrate their marriage in the church (RCIA, #47, National Statutes, #10). (See Policy 404.8.1, herein.)

Procedures

a) If two catechumens marry or a catechumen marries a non-Catholic Christian or unbaptized person, no dispensation needs to be granted for the catechumen. However the prenuptial questionnaire should still be completed and filed with other parish marriage records. It should be noted on the prenuptial questionnaire that the marriage involved a catechumen. Where there is doubt about the proper procedure, one should consult the Office of the Chancellor.

b) The same kind of pastoral care should be provided for catechumens preparing for marriage as for any individuals who marry in the church.

c) The marriage should be celebrated at a Liturgy of the Word. Chapter III of the *Rite of Marriage* is to be used.

d) The marriage should be properly recorded in the parish marriage record book and in the parish book of catechumens. (See §902.4, *Illegitimacy.*)

106.1.2 Policy *When a catechumen marries a Catholic, the Catholic party is required by church law to request a dispensation (disparity of cult). (See §300, Christian Marriage, Policy 304.11, herein.)*

Declarations of Nullity   §106.2

106.2.1 Policy *Non-baptized persons who need a declaration of nullity from their previous marriage are free to enter into the catechumenate. Such persons cannot, however, be accepted for the Rite of Election. Until the declaration of nullity is granted, candidates who need a declaration of nullity cannot be accepted for the Rite of Calling Candidates to Continuing Conversion. Pastoral staffs should uncover the need for a declaration of nullity through personal interviews early in the process. Non-baptized persons in need of a declaration of nullity who are received into the catechumenate must clearly understand at the outset that they may not be initiated at the approaching Easter.*

106.2.2 Policy *A catechumen or candidate who is divorced and not remarried and does not intend to remarry is not in need of a declaration of nullity to be accepted for the Rite of Election, the Rite of Calling the Candidates to Continuing Conversion, or, consequently, the sacraments of initiation. However, the implications of future attempts to remarry without a declaration of nullity must be carefully explained before the discernment for the rite is completed. Consultation on this matter and presentation of marriage cases should be made to the archdiocesan matrimonial tribunal, which is prepared to give special attention to these cases.*

§106.3   Validation of Marriages

106.3.1 Policy *When a marriage must be validated in the church, the validation ceremony shall take place prior to celebrating the initiation sacraments. One cannot enter the full sacramental life of the church unless one is completely free to receive the sacraments. It is pastorally advisable to validate the marriage in the church as early in the process as possible.*

§106.4   Marriage Preparation and Christian Initiation

106.4.1 Policy *When a catechumen or candidate is engaged to be married, the initiation process shall not be rushed merely to allow for initiation before the marriage is celebrated.*

Procedures

a) Because Christian marriage is a serious vocation, its preparation should not be neglected or weakened because of one's participation in the catechumenate. If it is not possible to participate fully in both processes, preparation to celebrate Christian marriage takes precedence over preparation for Christian initiation. It may be more appropriate to concentrate on the preparation for Christian marriage and postpone or extend the catechumenate.

b) It is always pastorally prudent and wise to refer the newly married couple to their respective pastor who can then assume the responsibility for seeing that the non-baptized person, catechumen, or candidate has the opportunity to complete their initiation.

c) Pastoral ministers are reminded that candidates (baptized non-Catholics) need not participate in a complete catechumenal process, as would catechumens (unbaptized persons). (See National Statutes, #30.)

Christian Burial of Catechumens and Candidates §106.5

106.5.1 Policy *Because they are already part of the household of Christ, catechumens and candidates have the right to Christian burial in the Catholic church. (See canon 1183; National Statutes, #9; and §701.1.c, Entitlement to Church's Ministry at Time of Death, herein.)*

Procedures

The funeral liturgy, including the funeral Mass, should be celebrated as usual, omitting only language referring directly to the sacraments which the catechumen or candidate has not received in the Catholic church. In view of the sensibilities of the immediate family of the deceased cat-echumen or candidate, the funeral Mass may be omitted (National Statutes, #9).

Orthodox Christian Candidates §106.6

106.6.1 Policy *Ordinarily, an Orthodox Christian can only be received into the corresponding Eastern Catholic church. It may be possible to obtain permission to be received into the Latin Rite.*

Procedures

Because of the extreme complexity and sensitivity of these pastoral issues, parish ministers should consult with the Office of the Chancellor.

§107

The Sacrament of Penance and Christian Initiation

Special Note: Although not a sacrament of initiation, there are often questions about celebrating the sacrament of penance in conjunction with the process of initiation. These policies are provided here for the sake of completeness.

§107.1 Candidates' Celebration of the Sacrament of Penance

107.1.1 Policy *Candidates are to receive a thorough catechesis on the sacrament of penance and are to be encouraged in the frequent celebration of the sacrament (National Statutes, #27, 36). They shall be invited to celebrate the sacrament of penance prior to their reception into full communion, but not at the same liturgy. Candidates are required to celebrate the sacrament of penance prior to their reception into the full communion of the Roman Catholic Church if they are guilty of serious sin. All candidates should be encouraged to do so in any case (RCIA, #482).*

§107.2 Catechumens' Celebration of the Sacrament of Penance

107.2.1 Policy *Catechumens preparing for baptism (both children and adults) do not celebrate the sacrament of penance prior to baptism. They are to be invited to participate in non-sacramental penitential rites as found in the RCIA, #291–303, so that they may come to understand the reality of sin and appreciate the comforting message of God's pardon.*

Children's Celebration of the Sacrament of Penance §107.3

107.3.1 Policy *Non-Catholic children who were baptized in infancy but are preparing for reception into the full communion of the Roman Catholic Church should be adequately prepared and encouraged to celebrate the sacrament of penance some time prior to their formal reception into the Catholic church (RCIA, #482, National Statutes, #27).*

RESOURCES

Official Documents

Rite of Christian Initiation of Adults

1. International Committee on English in the Liturgy [ICEL] and Bishops' Committee on the Liturgy [BCL]. *Liturgy Documentary Series 4: Christian Initiation of Adults*, revised. Washington: Office of Publishing Services, 1988. Publication No. 895 – 9.
2. ICEL & BCL. *Rite of Christian Initiation of Adults*, study edition. Chicago: Liturgy Training Publications, 1988.
3. BCL. *Study Text 10: Christian Initiation of Adults: A Commentary.* Washington: Office of Publishing Services, 1985. Pub. No. 934.

Infant Baptism

1. ICEL & BCL. *Rite of Baptism for Children.* New York: Catholic Book Publishing Company, 1977.

Rite of Penance

1. ICEL & BCL. *Liturgy Documentary Series 7: Penance and Reconciliation in the Church.* Washington: Office of Publishing and Promotion Services, 1986. Publication No. 104.
2. ICEL & BCL. *The Rite of Penance.* New York: Pueblo Publishing Company, 1975.

Rite of Marriage

1. ICEL & BCL. *The Rite of Marriage.* New York: Catholic Book Publishing Company, 1970.

National and International Guidelines

1. *Catechism of the Catholic Church.* Libreria Editrice Vaticana, 1992.
2. International Council for Catechesis. *Adult Catechesis in the Christian Community.* Washington: USCC, 1992.
3. National Conference of Catholic Bishops [NCCB]. *Sharing the Light of Faith: National Catechetical Directory for the Catholics of the United States.* Washington: USCC, 1979.

Archdiocesan Guidelines

1. *Religious Education Policies.* Archdiocese of Chicago: Office of Religious Education, 1990.
2. *Responses to Frequently Asked Questions on the Christian Initiation of Adults and Children of Catechetical Age for the Province of Chicago.* Catholic Conference of Illinois, 1991.

§200

THE SUNDAY EUCHARIST AND OTHER LITURGIES

∎

contents

§200

THE SUNDAY EUCHARIST AND OTHER LITURGIES

Introduction

The Christian community has the right and obligation to pray, even when a priest is not present to preside over the assembly. "Public and common prayer among the people of God is rightly considered to be among the primary duties of the church" (*General Instruction on the Liturgy of the Hours*, #1).

The church at prayer gives witness to the world of its relationship with God. "The excellence of Christian prayer lies in this, that it shares in the very love of the only begotten Son for the Father and in that prayer that the Son put into words in his earthly life and which still continues unceasingly in the name of the human race for its salvation, throughout the universal church and in all its members" (*General Instruction on the Liturgy of the Hours*, #7).

§201 Sunday Eucharist: The Source and Summit of the Christian Life

While there are a number of ways in which the church gathers in prayer, the Sunday eucharist is the apex of the church's life of worship. All other forms of communal prayer, including daily Mass, flow from the celebration of the Mass on the Lord's day. Sunday Mass is clearly the ideal in light of which all other celebrations are to be understood (*Catechism of the Catholic Church*, #1322–1344).

Sunday, the day of the Lord's resurrection, the "eighth day" on which creation was made new, has a rich, even sacramental significance. When the church gathers on Sunday to celebrate the eucharist, it enters into the paschal mystery most fully and expresses its identity as the Body of Christ most completely. The daily worship of the church flows out of its celebration of eucharist on Sunday.

As the source and summit of the Christian life, the eucharist both expresses and reinforces the church's nature and mission. It is in the Mass that we most perfectly express our identity as members of the Body of Christ and renew our commitment to be a leaven in the world.

Due to its mysterious, symbolic nature, though, the meaning of the eucharist cannot be defined simply or expressed adequately in words. It is a multi-dimensional, multi-faceted reality that must be approached from a variety of perspectives in order to appreciate it in its fullness.

The Mass memorializes Christ's last supper with his disciples; it is the sacrament of Christ's great paschal sacrifice, his victory over sin and death; it is the church's participation in Christ's real presence; it is the new and everlasting covenant of grace wherein we pledge ourselves to live as Christ's disciples; and it is the foretaste and promise of the heavenly banquet.

Because the eucharist is better understood as an action than as an object, the liturgical celebration of the Mass must be the model for our discussion of the eucharist. To talk about the eucharistic elements of bread and wine transformed into the body and blood of Christ, apart from the liturgical action of the gathered assembly, is to risk speaking of the eucharist out of context.

St. Paul writes in 1 Corinthians 11:23–26,

> I received from the Lord what I handed on to you, namely, that the Lord Jesus on the night in which he was betrayed took bread, and after he had given thanks, broke it and said, 'This is my body, which is for you. Do this in remembrance of me.' In the same way, after the supper, he took the cup, saying, 'This cup is the new covenant in my blood. Do this, whenever you drink it, in remembrance of me.' Every time, then, you eat this bread and drink this cup, you proclaim the death of the Lord until he comes!

In this early scriptural evidence of our eucharistic tradition, we have expressed for us the liturgical shape and sacramental significance the eucharist was to take: the Lord took bread, gave thanks, broke the bread and gave it to his disciples; when we eat and drink of it, we proclaim his death until he comes. The eucharist is a ritual action in which Christ's paschal victory is signified, so that through participation in the eucharistic action believers of every age are made sharers in Christ's victory over sin and death.

This paschal victory of Christ which is signified in the Mass is the church's most treasured memory. It is the very source of its existence and the promise of its destiny. Although sometimes understood to refer narrowly to the Lord's death and resurrection, the paschal mystery must be more broadly seen to include Christ's role in all of salvation history: from his eternal co-existence with the Father, through his incarnation, life, passion and death, to his victorious resurrection, ascension and longed-for return.

By the power of the Holy Spirit, when the church "memorializes" these saving deeds of Christ in the Mass, their power and grace are made present to us again. The Fathers of the church spoke of this mystery as "a holy exchange": Christ, by participating in our humanity, makes us sharers in his divinity through our access to the sacraments of the church and, most especially, through the eucharistic action.

The *General Instruction of the Roman Missal, #1* begins with a clear statement on the importance of the Mass:

> The celebration of Mass is the action of Christ and the people of God hierarchically assembled. For both the universal and the local church, and for each person, it is the center of the whole Christian life. The Mass reaches the high point of the action by which God in Christ sanctifies the world and the high point of men's worship of the Father, as they adore him through Christ, His Son. During the course of the year the mysteries of redemption are recalled at Mass so that they are in some way made present. All other actions and works of the Christian are related to the eucharistic celebration, leading up to it and flowing from it.

Thus, the eucharist is the preeminent celebration of what it means to be, to become and to build up the church.

§201.1 Utmost Care in Preparation and Celebration

201.1.1 Policy *The Sunday eucharist, as the preeminent gathering of the local community, requires the utmost care in preparation and celebration. This care shall be reflected in the amount of time given to its preparation and the financial resources budgeted for its celebration.*

Respect for the Role of Each Participant §201.2

201.2.1 Policy *Everyone in the eucharistic assembly has the right and duty to take his or her part according to their proper role in the assembly. Accordingly, the appropriate ministerial roles are to be filled by the faithful at each celebration of Mass. This includes music, which is normative for Sunday celebrations (GIRM, #58–64).*

Communion Services and Sunday or Holy Day Masses §201.3

201.3.1 Policy *Since there are adequate numbers of clergy that could be available to celebrate Sunday or Holy Day Masses in the archdiocese of Chicago, the parish is not free to schedule a communion service instead of Mass on Sundays, Saturday Masses of anticipation, or Holy Days.*

§202

Mass Schedules

§202.1 The Integrity of Catholic Worship

202.1.1 Policy *Liturgical celebrations include effective preaching, well-prepared ministers, quality music, an appropriate environment and an active assembly — all in harmony with the particular liturgical feasts and seasons. Pastoral staffs shall ensure that these elements are present at each Sunday liturgy (cf. General Instruction of the Roman Missal; Introduction to the Lectionary; Constitution on the Sacred Liturgy).*

Procedures

a) Parish staffs, in collaboration with the liturgy committee and the parish pastoral council, are to make a thorough periodic review of parish liturgies in light of the *General Instruction of the Roman Missal;* the *Introduction to the Lectionary;* the *Constitution on the Sacred Liturgy; Environment and Art in Catholic Worship;* and *Music in Catholic Worship.*

b) When assistance is needed or desired, the pastoral staff is encouraged to consult with the Office for Divine Worship.

> **Documentation** *"After due regard to the nature and circumstances of each assembly, the [eucharistic] celebration is planned in such way that it brings about in the faithful a participation in body and spirit that is conscious, active, full, and motivated by faith, hope, and charity. The church desires this kind of participation, the nature of the celebration demands it, and for the Christian people it is a right and duty they have by reason of their baptism"* (General Instruction of the Roman Missal, #3).
>
> *"The responsibility for effective pastoral celebration in a parish community falls upon all who exercise major roles in the liturgy. The practical preparation for each liturgical celebration should be done in a spirit of cooperation by all parties*

concerned, under the guidance of the rector of the church, whether it be ritual, pastoral, or musical matters" (Music in Catholic Worship, #10).

"To promote active participation, the people should be encouraged to take part by means of verbal expression of praise, responses, the singing of psalms, antiphons, and songs, as well as by actions, gestures, and bodily attitudes. And at the proper times all should observe a reverent silence" (Constitution on the Sacred Liturgy, #30).

General Principles for Determining the Number of Masses   §202.2

202.2.1 Policy In order that the integrity of the liturgy be preserved in our parishes, the following shall be balanced in determining the number of Masses: (a) providing Masses so that the faithful can fulfill their Sunday obligation; (b) enabling the members of a parish to gather as one worshiping community (to the extent this is feasible); (c) celebrating liturgies that are well prepared and include music and the full complement of ministries; and (d) not overextending the priest presiders and other liturgical ministers.

202.2.2 Policy Parish staffs shall evaluate the necessity of any Sunday Mass at which the attendance is consistently less than 50% of the seating capacity of the church. When this is the case, unless there is a special need (i.e., for a particular ethnic group within the parish) or the congregation cannot be accommodated at another Mass, that Sunday Mass shall be either eliminated or combined with another. Certain parish communities have churches that are larger than the needs of the community. This calls for a review of the worship space to see whether the space can be altered to more appropriately accommodate the size of the congregation.

§202.3   Catechesis for Change

202.3.1 Policy *If in the pastoral judgment of the pastoral staff, in consultation with the parish pastoral council and liturgy committee, the weekend Mass schedule is to be changed, education and explanation shall be given to the parish community.*

§202.4   Multicultural Sensitivity

202.4.1 Policy *Pastoral leaders in multicultural parishes shall respond effectively to the special needs of the people, particularly when important changes are occurring within the parish population. The celebration of the liturgy shall reflect the ethnic composition of the parish including language, music and artistic considerations.*

§202.5   Weekend Evening Masses

202.5.1 Policy *Any Mass scheduled for Saturday or Sunday evening shall meet a definite pastoral need and be planned and carried out with the same quality and liturgical integrity as the other Sunday Masses.*

§202.6   Time Between Masses

202.6.1 Policy *Ordinarily, there shall be a minimum of one hour and thirty minutes between the starting times of Masses.*

Procedures

In setting the Sunday schedule, consideration should be given to allowing enough time for other rites which are celebrated in the Sunday liturgy (i.e., infant baptism, anointing of the sick, rites of the catechumenate, commissioning ministers, etc.). The length of time between Masses should ensure that no one is rushed — the priest, liturgical ministers or assembly — before, during or after the liturgy.

> **Documentation** *"As to the hours and the number of Masses to be celebrated in parishes, the convenience of the parish community must be kept in mind and the number of Masses not so multiplied as to harm pastoral effectiveness. Such would be the case, for example, if because there were too many Masses, only small groups of the faithful would attend each one in churches that can hold many people; or if, also because of the number of Masses, the priest were to be so overwhelmed with the work that they could fulfill their ministry only with great difficulty"* (Instruction on Worship of the Eucharist, #26).
>
> *"Among the symbols with which the liturgy deals, none is more important than [the] assembly of believers . . . The most powerful experience of the sacred is found in the celebration and the persons celebrating, that is, it is found in the action of the assembly: the living words, the living gestures, the living sacrifice, the living meal"* (Environment and Art in Catholic Worship, #28 – 29).
>
> *" 'In virtue of baptism, there is neither Jew nor Greek, slave nor free, male nor female, but all are one in Christ Jesus' (Gal 3:28). Therefore the assembly that most fully manifests the nature of the church in the eucharist is one in which the faithful of every class, age and condition are joined together . . . The best example of this unity is found in the full, active participation of all God's holy people . . . in the same eucharist, in a single prayer, at one altar at which the bishop presides, surrounded by his college of priests and by his ministers"* (Instruction on Worship of the Eucharist, #16).

202.6.2 Policy *In order to keep the proper focus on Sunday as the day of gathering for the eucharist, each parish may have one Saturday vigil liturgy for fulfilling the Sunday obligation.*

Procedures

a) The tradition of a vigil before a major feast has long been part of the liturgical practice of the church. A Saturday evening liturgy is considered a vigil Mass for the Sunday.

b) If a wedding is celebrated at a regularly scheduled Saturday vigil liturgy or at a regularly scheduled Sunday liturgy, the Sunday liturgy prevails.

Documentation *"When permission has been granted by the Apostolic See to fulfill the Sunday obligation on the preceding Saturday evening, pastors should explain to the faithful and should ensure that the significance of Sunday is not hereby obscured. The purpose of this concession is in fact to enable the Christians of today to celebrate more easily the day of the resurrection of the Lord.*

All concessions and contrary customs notwithstanding, when celebrated on Saturday this Mass may be celebrated only in the evening, at times determined by the local ordinary.

In these cases, the Mass celebrated is that assigned in the calendar to Sunday; the homily and the prayer of the faithful are not to be omitted.

What has been said above is equally valid for the Mass on Holy Days of Obligation which for the same reason has been transferred to the preceding evening" (Instruction on Worship of the Eucharist, #28).

§202.7 Time for Vigil Liturgies

202.7.1 Policy *The time for the vigil liturgy is ordinarily between 5:00 PM and 7:00 PM, but not earlier than 4:00 PM.*

Documentation *"Whenever the community gathers to celebrate the eucharist, it shows forth the death and resurrection of the Lord in the hope of his glorious coming. But the Sunday assembly shows this best of all, for this is the day of the week on which the Lord rose from the dead and on which, from apostolic tradition, the paschal mystery is celebrated in the eucharist in a special way . . . On this day above all, gathered as one, they are to hear the word of God and share in the paschal mystery"* (Instruction on Worship of the Eucharist, #25).

"The liturgical day runs from midnight to midnight, but the observance of Sunday and solemnities begins with the evening of the preceding day. The church

celebrates the paschal mystery on the first day of the week, known as the Lord's Day or Sunday. This follows a tradition handed down from the apostles and having its origin from the day of Christ's resurrection. Thus, Sunday must be ranked as the first Holy Day of all" (General Norms for the Liturgical Year and the Calendar, #3 – 4).

Easter Vigil §202.8

202.8.1 Policy While it fulfills the Sunday obligation, the Easter Vigil is not to be considered a Mass of anticipation for Easter but a unique liturgical experience in its own right. It shall not be celebrated until it is dark.

Documentation "The entire celebration of the Easter Vigil takes place at night. It should not begin before nightfall; it should end before daybreak on Sunday" (Roman Missal).

Saturday Morning Mass §202.9

202.9.1 Policy Because of an intensive offering of liturgical services on a weekend, when a vigil Mass is celebrated, no more than one Saturday morning Mass is to be regularly scheduled. This does not include weddings or funerals.

Weekday Masses §202.10

202.10.1 Policy On weekdays there shall not be more regularly scheduled Masses than there are priests assigned to the parish. A parish is not required to offer more than one daily Mass regardless of the number of priests assigned to the parish.

202.10.2 Policy *For a just cause, when there is only one priest assigned to a parish it is permissible to regularly eliminate Mass on one of the weekdays. When a priest is ill or must absent himself from the parish for several days, for example, for a retreat, clergy convocation or vacation, there is no obligation to provide the daily Mass.*

Procedures

a) The Mass schedules of neighboring parishes ought to be published for the convenience of the faithful.

b) Especially when Mass can not be celebrated, the faithful should be encouraged to gather for Morning Prayer or Evening Prayer or a Liturgy of the Word (See §205, The Liturgy of the Hours, herein).

c) Communion services are permitted in conformity with the principles issued in §206, Weekday Communion Services.

§202.11   Communion Services

202.11.1 Policy *In the archdiocese of Chicago, communion services are not permitted on Sundays even if one of the regularly scheduled Masses is canceled. (See also Policy 201.3.1 and §206, Weekday Communion Services, herein)*

Documentation *"No Christian Community is every built up unless it has its roots and center in the eucharistic liturgy." Therefore, before the bishop decides on having Sunday assemblies without celebration of the eucharist, the following in addition to the status of parishes (see no. 5) should be considered: the possibility of recourse to priests, even religious priests, who are not directly assigned to the care of souls and the frequency of Masses in the various parishes and churches. The preeminence of the celebration of the eucharist, particularly on Sunday, over other pastoral activities is to be respected (Instruction on Worship of the Eucharist, #25).*

"Whenever and wherever Mass cannot be celebrated on Sunday the first thing to be ascertained is whether the faithful can go to a church in a place nearby to participate there in the eucharistic mystery. At the present time this solution is to be

recommended and to be retained where it is in effect; but it demands that the faithful, rightly imbued with a fuller understanding of the Sunday assembly, respond with good will to a new situation" (Directory for Sunday Celebrations in the Absence of a Priest, #18).

     Regarding the use of communion services, the Directory makes clear: "It is imperative that the faithful be taught to see the substitutional character of these celebrations, which should not be regarded as the optimal solution to new difficulties nor as a surrender to mere convenience. Therefore a gathering or assembly of this kind can never be held on a Sunday in places where Mass has already been celebrated or is to be celebrated or was celebrated in a different language. Nor is it right to have more than one assembly of this kind on any given Sunday" (Directory for Sunday Celebrations in the Absence of a Priest, #21).

Sacrament of Penance §202.12

202.12.1 Policy *The sacrament of penance or any other service shall not be celebrated while Mass is being celebrated in the same space. Regularly scheduled confessions between Sunday Masses are not permitted.*

Procedures

The parish staff, in consultation with the community, should evaluate the schedule for the celebration of the sacrament of penance before the Saturday vigil liturgy to ensure that there is adequate time to prepare for the eucharist. It is recommended that the presider of the vigil liturgy be someone other than the confessor.

Simultaneous Masses at Same Location §202.13

202.13.1 Policy *Only one Mass may be regularly celebrated at the same time on parish grounds except when the size of the church is not able to accommodate all who come to worship. Any fragmentation of the community should be avoided.*

Procedures

Mass schedules arranged in years past may have allowed for overflow Masses. If the necessity of this duplication still exists, permission should be obtained from the Office of the Chancellor.

> **Documentation** "*The scattering of the people that generally occurs when Masses are celebrated at the same time in the same church should be carefully avoided on Sundays and Holy Days of Obligation*" (Instruction on Worship of the Eucharist, #17).

§202.14 Distinctive Communities of Worship

***202.14.1 Policy** A parish Mass schedule shall neither exclude special groups from joining the parish assembly nor preclude the opportunity for them to gather as a distinctive community for Sunday eucharist.*

Procedures

a) Parishes with special interest group liturgies are to evaluate the genuine need for them in light of present needs and human resources. The value of their participation in the mainstream of parish liturgical life is to be fostered.

b) All liturgical celebrations should be inclusive of children.

c) It is more desirable for children to attend a parish Sunday liturgy than to provide a special Mass for them. It may be desirable on occasion to plan the parish liturgy with the particular needs of the children or teens in mind. Celebrating a separate Liturgy of the Word for children is permissible. In this case the children are dismissed from the assembly after the opening prayer and return to the assembly for the Liturgy of the eucharist. The Liturgy of the Word for children is not a catechetical session but a liturgical experience.

d) In parishes where weekend Masses are celebrated in more than one language, every effort should be made to celebrate multilingual liturgies on the great feasts when parish unity is most appropriately fostered. This is especially true during the Triduum.

Documentation *"Pastors have the responsibility of providing suitable ways to assist the faithful from other regions to join with the local community. This should be of particular concern in the churches of large cities. . . . Where there are many visitors or expatriates of another language, pastors should provide them with the opportunity, at least occasionally, to participate in the Mass celebrated in the way customary for them"* (Instruction on Worship of the Eucharist, #19).

"Often the problem of diversity can be mitigated by supplementing the parish Sunday celebration with special celebrations for smaller homogeneous groups. 'The needs of the faithful of a particular cultural background or of a particular age level may often be met by a music that can serve as a congenial, liturgically oriented expression of prayer.' . . . Celebration in such groups, 'in which the genuine sense of community is more readily experienced, can contribute significantly to growth in awareness of the parish as community, especially when all the faithful participate in the parish Mass on the Lord's Day.' Nevertheless, it would be out of harmony with the Lord's will for unity in his church if believers were to worship only in such homogeneous groupings" (Music in Catholic Worship, #18).

"So that the unity of the parish community may stand out in the eucharist on Sundays and Holy Days, Masses for such particular groups as parish societies should, if possible, preferably be held on weekdays. If they cannot be transferred to weekdays, care should be taken to maintain the unity of the parish community by incorporating these particular groups into the parish celebrations" (Instruction on Worship of the Eucharist, #27).

"Pastoral care also has as its purpose and direction particular groups. This is not for the sake of creating ecclesiolae or privilege, but to serve the faithful's particular needs or to deepen the Christian life in accord with the requirements and capacities of the members of these groups. This brings advantages that spring from a special spiritual or apostolic, common bond and from the desire to help one another toward spiritual growth. From experience pastoral activity teaches how much good having their own celebrations can do for these groups. When these celebrations have proper and wise direction, they are no obstacle to parish unity; instead they serve the parish's missionary activity by their power to achieve closer contact with some of the people or to deepen the formation of others" (Instruction on Masses with Special Groups).

"If the place itself and the nature of the community permit, it will be appropriate to celebrate the liturgy of the word, including a homily, with the children in a separate, but not too distant, room. Then, before the eucharistic liturgy begins, the children are led to the place where the adults have meanwhile celebrated their own Liturgy of the Word . . . With the consent of the pastor or rector of the church, one of the adults may speak to the children after the gospel, especially if the priest finds it difficult to adapt himself to the mentality of the children" (Directory for Masses with Children, #17, 24).

§202.15 Place for Mass

202.15.1 Policy *Every Sunday Mass shall be celebrated in a dignified, suitable place. Normally this will be the church.*

Procedures

a) The principles outlined in *Environment and Art in Catholic Worship* are the norms governing worship space.

b) Parish communities undertaking a review of weekend liturgies are encouraged to assess the appropriateness of their worship space.

§202.16 Access for Persons with Disabilities

202.16.1 Policy *Provision shall be made for easy access for the elderly and those with physical disabilities.*

Documentation *"For the celebration of the eucharist, the people of God are normally assembled in a church or, if there is none, in some other place worthy of this great mystery"* (General Instruction of the Roman Missal, #253).

"As common prayer and ecclesial experience, liturgy flourishes in a climate of hospitality: a situation in which people are comfortable with one another, either knowing or being introduced to one another; a space in which people are seated together, with mobility, in view of one another as well as the focal points of the rite, involved as participants and not as spectators" (Environment and Art in Catholic Worship, #11).

"In most cases the eucharistic celebration for groups is to be held in a place of worship. The faculty of allowing a eucharistic celebration for special groups to take place outside a place of worship is reserved to the local ordinary" (Instruction on Masses with Special Groups, #3,4).

Faculty to Celebrate More Than One Mass §202.17

202.17.1 Policy *For a just cause, a priest is permitted to celebrate Mass twice on any given day. If pastoral necessity requires, he is permitted to celebrate a third Mass on Sundays and Holy Days of Obligation.*

Documentation *"It is not licit for a priest to celebrate the eucharist more than once a day except for certain instances when the law permits such celebration or concelebration more than once" (canon 905, §1).*

"If priests are lacking, the local ordinary may permit priests, for a just cause, to celebrate twice a day and even, if pastoral need requires it, three times on Sundays and Holy Days of Obligation" (canon 905, §2).

Liturgical Ministers §202.18

202.18.1 Policy *Ordinarily, a lay liturgical minister shall serve at only one Sunday Mass.*

Procedures

a) It may be necessary in some parishes to extend to more people the opportunity to serve as liturgical ministers, according to liturgical norms, so that ordinarily each will serve at and participate fully in only one Mass. This allows individuals to give their full energy and attention to serving the assembly.

b) The selection of liturgical ministers should be made in conformity with the universal norms of the church and be inclusive of all men, women and children and reflect the ages and ethnic and racial composition of the community.

Documentation *"The liturgical assembly truly requires readers, even those not instituted. Proper measures must therefore be taken to ensure that there are* *qualified lay persons who have been trained to carry out this ministry. Whenever there is more than one reading, it is better to assign the readings to different readers, if available"* (Introduction to Lectionary for Mass, #52).

"It is desirable that as a rule an acolyte, a reader and a cantor assist the priest celebrant" (General Instruction on the Roman Missal, #78).

"In liturgical celebrations each person, minister or layman, who has an office to perform, should do all of, but only, those parts which pertain to his office by the nature of the rite and the norms of liturgy" (Constitution on the Sacred Liturgy, #28).

§203

Mass Offerings

Ordinary Offering for Celebration of a Mass   §203.1

203.1.1 Policy *The custom of giving offerings to have Masses said for specific intentions is a laudable one and shall be maintained as much as possible.*

Procedures

The faithful should be catechized about the theological meaning of the offering given for the celebration of the Mass and on the ascetical importance of almsgiving and the sharing of goods, of which the offerings for the celebration of the Mass are an outstanding form (See Art. 7, "On Collective Mass Intentions," Congregation for the Clergy, Feb. 22, 1991).

> **Documentation** *"In the established tradition of the church, the faithful, moved by an ecclesial and religious sense, join to the eucharistic sacrifice a kind of sacrifice of their own, as a way of taking part more intensely. They thus do their share to provide for the church's needs, especially the support of its ministers. This practice is in accord with the spirit of the Lord's words: 'The laborer . . . is worthy of his hire' (Luke 10:7), which St. Paul alludes to in 1 Timothy 5:18 and in 1 Corinthians 9:7 – 14" (Pope Paul VI, motu proprio Firma in Traditione, June 13, 1974: AAS 66 (1974), 308 – 311).*
> *See also canons 952, §1 and 1264, §2.*

203.1.2 Policy *Consistent with the determination of the bishops of the Province of Chicago, the ordinary offering to be made for the celebration and application of a Mass in the archdiocese of Chicago is $10 (canon 952, §1). Any amount contributed in excess of the customary offering may be given to charity or deposited in the general funds of the parish.*

Procedures

a) **Bination.** Unlike the 1917 Code, the present law allows a priest to accept offerings for any number of Masses he celebrates on one day, as long as he does not personally retain more than one offering (except on Christmas Day, when he may retain three). Amounts received beyond one offering may be given to charity or deposited in the general funds of the parish.

b) **Concelebration.** An offering may be accepted for concelebration if that is the only Mass a priest celebrates that day (canon 945, §1). If a priest who concelebrates also celebrates another Mass that day, he may not accept an offering for the concelebration even if he were to give the offering to charity (canon 951, §2). However, if a priest is the principal celebrant at a concelebrated Mass the norms for bination apply (canon 951, §1).

c) **Missa Pro Populo.** A pastor or parochial administrator is obligated to celebrate the *Missa pro populo* every Sunday and Holy Day of obligation, and he may not accept an offering for this. If he is legitimately prevented from this celebration, he is to delegate another priest to say the *Missa pro populo* on those days or he is to say it himself on other days (canons 534, §1; 540, §1). The pastor or parochial administrator may, however, retain a Mass offering for a second Mass which he celebrates on the same day as the *Missa pro populo* (canon 951, §1).

> **Documentation** *"Separate Masses shall be applied for the intentions for which an individual offering, even if small, has been made and accepted" (canon 948). The priest who accepts such offerings is bound in justice to satisfy the obligations personally or by committing them to another (canons 949, 954–55).*

§203.2 Collective Mass Intentions   §203.2

203.2.1 Policy *The faithful are free to combine their intentions and offerings for the celebration of a single Mass. Masses with "collective" intentions are permissible when the following circumstances have been met:*
1) *the people making the offering have been previously explicitly informed and have freely consented to having their intention and offering combined with another in a single offering of Mass;*
2) *the place and time for the celebration of the particular Mass is made public.*

Procedures

As is the case with Masses offered for individual intentions and offerings (Policy 203.1.2, herein), when Masses for collective intentions are celebrated in the archdiocese of Chicago, any amount contributed in excess of the customary offering may be given to charity or deposited in the general funds of the parish.

203.2.3 Policy *No more than two Masses with "collective" intentions and offerings shall be offered during any given week.*

Documentation *See "On Collective Mass Intentions," Decree of the Congregation for the Clergy, Feb. 22, 1991.*

Offerings for Weddings and Funerals   §203.3

203.3.1 Policy *Consistent with the determination of the bishops of the Province of Chicago, the limit on the offerings given on the occasion of administering sacraments and sacramentals is $500 for weddings and $150 for funerals, exclusive of expenses (canon 1264, §2).*

Procedures

The term "limit" as used herein indicates the maximum donation that a parish in the archdiocese of Chicago and other dioceses of Illinois may accept for a funeral or wedding. A person's inability to make an offering would not preclude their receiving the Sacrament of Matrimony or the Rite of Christian Burial.

§204

Auxiliary Ministers of Holy Communion at Mass and in Service to the Sick

In response to a pastoral need, in 1969 Pope Paul VI issued the instruction *Custos Fidei,* which allows baptized members of the faithful to assist in the distribution of Holy Communion in certain pastoral circumstances. This instruction and subsequent documentation, including *Immensae Caritatis* (1973) and the fourth edition of the *General Instruction of the Roman Missal* (1975), has resulted in making the practice of auxiliary (or extraordinary or special) ministers of Holy Communion at Mass and to the sick a common pastoral practice in the United States.

The ordinary ministers of the eucharist are bishops, priests and deacons and formally installed acolytes. They exercise this ministry by virtue of their ordination or installation by the bishop.

The purpose of auxiliary ministers of communion at Mass is to assist at the distribution of Holy Communion when the number of ordinary ministers of the eucharist is insufficient to serve the assembly in a reverent manner. Assigning auxiliary ministers prevents the communion rite from becoming excessively long and out of proportion to the rest of the liturgy. Auxiliary ministers of Holy Communion are especially useful when communion is offered under the forms of both bread and wine.

The purpose of auxiliary or special ministers of communion to the sick or homebound is to extend the church's love and concern for the sick and homebound by a personal visit that includes the celebration of the Rite of Holy Communion Outside of Mass. Auxiliary ministers of communion to the sick are called upon when the parish priest or deacon is not able to adequately attend to the needs of the sick or in a hospital or religious institution where priests or deacons are not available.

In the archdiocese of Chicago, the policy authorizing the practice of auxiliary ministers of communion at Mass was first promulgated by John Cardinal Cody on July 4, 1971. The policy authorizing the practice of auxiliary ministers of communion to the sick was promulgated on June 22, 1973. These policies and procedures reaffirm the original authorization of this pastoral practice and provide additional policies and procedures for good order and pastoral practice in the archdiocese of Chicago. These policies and procedures apply to parishes and all Catholic institutions such as hospitals, nursing homes, schools and convents.

In the archdiocese of Chicago, the ministries of auxiliary ministers of communion at Mass and auxiliary ministers of communion to the sick are regarded as two distinct ministries. Each ministry presumes a distinct formation and mandate. However, an individual may be mandated for both ministries.

§204.1   Selection of Ministers

204.1.1 Policy *The selection of auxiliary ministers of communion at Mass or for the sick shall be made under the direction of the pastor, or the superior or the director of the religious institution.*

204.1.2 Policy *Auxiliary ministers of communion at Mass or for the sick shall be baptized and confirmed Roman Catholics who regularly share in the eucharist. They shall be of exemplary Christian character, committed to the faith, devoted to the eucharist, respected by the community, and demonstrate an interest and involvement in the community's life. They may be as young as high school age, provided they are deemed responsible to carry out the mandate entrusted to them.*

Procedures

a) Pastors, superiors and directors of religious institutions charged with the responsibility of selecting auxiliary ministers of communion should invite the collaboration of others who exercise pastoral leadership in the community in the selection of auxiliary ministers of communion.

b) The invitation to be an auxiliary minister of communion is not to be understood as a reward but as a call to service. In addition to what is already stated in Policy 204.1.2, the one selected should be spiritually sound and capable of adhering to all of the community's procedures for communion ministers.

Preparation and Formation §204.2

204.2.1 Policy *Auxiliary ministers of communion at Mass shall receive adequate catechesis and liturgical training before they are mandated to exercise their ministry.*

Procedures

a) Catechesis and liturgical training for auxiliary ministers of communion at Mass is provided by the local community.

b) Catechesis should include an appreciation for one's baptism and solidarity with the church, an understanding of the eucharist, and an understanding of the significance of this extraordinary ministry.

c) The auxiliary minister's liturgical training should include very specific instruction on the order and practice of distributing Holy Communion in the community.

d) Assistance for catechesis and liturgical training is available through the Office for Divine Worship.

e) Every community is responsible for the formation and spiritual enrichment of mandated communion ministers.

204.2.2 Policy *Communion ministers to the sick receive catechesis and pastoral and liturgical training that is distinct from the formation and training of auxiliary ministers of communion at Mass. This catechesis and formation shall be completed before communion ministers to the sick are formally mandated.*

Procedures

a) Catechesis for communion ministers to the sick is provided through the Office for Divine Worship.

b) A community or several communities in collaboration with one another may conduct their own program of preparing communion ministers to the sick by submitting an outline of their program for approval by the Office for Divine Worship.

c) The Office for Divine Worship can provide assistance and guidance for planning the catechesis and the pastoral and liturgical training of ministers to the sick.

§204.3 Mandation and Commission

204.3.1 Policy *Pastors, superiors and directors of Catholic institutions shall submit the names of those who are to be mandated as auxiliary ministers of communion at Mass and/or for the sick to the director of the Office for Divine Worship.*

Procedures

a) Auxiliary ministers of communion at Mass and/or for the sick are mandated for a period of three years. This allows for a local review of all communion ministers requesting a renewal of mandated persons.

b) All parishes, religious communities and other Catholic institutions have been divided alphabetically into three cycles. Communion ministers mandated within the local institutional cycle must be renewed when the community's cycle is due for renewal. Notification for renewal is sent by the Office for Divine Worship.

c) Communion ministers mandated in another diocese can be accepted for service by the approval of the pastor, local superior or institution director. Their mandate must be renewed when the parish or institution submits or resubmits names for mandation at the time their cycle is due.

d) An individual cannot request on his or her own behalf to be mandated. They can only be recommended by the pastor or authorized superior.

204.3.2 Policy *After receiving a mandate through the Office for Divine Worship, auxiliary ministers of communion at Mass or to the sick shall be commissioned in the local community where they serve.*

Procedures

a) The rite of commissioning is found in the *Book of Blessings*, chapter 63.

b) Those who are mandated may receive their certificates at the rite of commissioning.

c) Once mandated, auxiliary ministers of communion at Mass or to the sick may exercise their ministry anywhere in the archdiocese of Chicago, provided the local pastor or superior of the place has given explicit permission.

204.3.3 Policy *In cases of immediate pastoral need, priests with faculties in the archdiocese of Chicago may mandate an individual for a particular occasion (see Policy 803.3).*

§204.4   Service at the Altar

204.4.1 Policy *Auxiliary ministers of communion at Mass shall only serve when there are insufficient numbers of bishops, priests or deacons present to assist in the distribution of communion or when the ordinary ministers are prevented from doing so, for example, because of physical disability or participation in some other ministry (Congregation for Sacraments, June 15, 1987).*

> **Special Note:** *Availability in this case presumes that all who administer communion have been notified and assigned prior to the liturgy so that good order is observed. This is especially important in special gatherings where ministers may not be familiar with the local procedures for distributing communion on those occasions.*

204.4.2 Policy *Auxiliary ministers of communion at Mass shall not be vested in any special garb, but shall dress neatly in a manner befitting the dignity of serving the community at the celebration of the eucharist.*

Procedures

a) Seating in the assembly is preferred to seating next to the altar.

b) Communion ministers do not ordinarily participate in the entrance procession.

204.4.3 Policy *The presider shall receive communion before distributing the consecrated bread and wine to the communion ministers and the assembly. However, auxiliary ministers of communion may receive communion after the assembly has received.*

204.4.4 Policy *Communion ministers do not self-communicate, but receive communion from another minister.*

Procedures

Communion ministers may receive communion from another minister at the altar or at a side station.

204.4.5 Policy *The proper and only permissible form for distributing Holy Communion is to offer the consecrated bread by saying, "The Body of Christ" and to offer the consecrated wine by saying, "The Blood of Christ." No other words shall be added and the formula shall not be edited.*

Procedures

a) The communion minister may address the communicant by name before saying, "The Body of Christ" or "The Blood of Christ."

b) Special blessings for children or infants are not recommended while distributing communion. Children and infants are blessed with the full assembly at the end of Mass.

c) All auxiliary ministers of communion should be prepared for serving the consecrated bread and the consecrated wine and willing to distribute either form depending on the need.

d) Although intinction is permitted, it is not recommended because it eliminates the possibility of receiving communion in the hand and has, moreover, a minimal sign value (*This Holy and Living Sacrifice*, #44).

e) If intinction is chosen, it is the minister and not the communicant who dips the host into the chalice (*This Holy and Living Sacrifice*, #52).

f) If the eucharistic bread or any particle of it should fall, it is to be picked up reverently by the communion minister. The consecrated bread may be consumed by the minister or completely dissolved in water before being poured into the sacrarium. If any of the consecrated wine spills, the area should be washed and the water poured into the sacrarium.

204.4.6 Policy *Whatever consecrated wine may remain after the distribution of holy communion shall be consumed by the ministers. A small quantity may be saved for taking communion to the sick who cannot take solid food, if this is to take place the same day. The consecrated wine is never reserved for another Mass, nor is it poured into the sacrarium.*

Procedures

a) Communion ministers clean and purify the vessels after Mass, or if necessary, after communion, in the sacristy.

b) If the cups are to be purified after Mass, the cups should be covered with a purificator or other cloth until the cups are washed.

§204.5 Service to the Sick

204.5.1 Policy *Communion ministers to the sick shall use the rites provided by the church in "Pastoral Care of the Sick" when ministering to the sick or homebound at home or in a hospital.*

204.5.2 Policy *The Holy Eucharist shall be carried to the sick in a pyx provided for this purpose by the pastor or superior. The eucharist is never carried in a handkerchief, envelope, etc. Nor is the Blessed Sacrament ever reserved in private homes, offices or automobiles.*

Procedures

a) Arrangements need to be made with the parish or institution for obtaining access to the tabernacle so that the reserved eucharist can be carried to the sick when needed.

b) Those who care for the sick and infirm should be instructed to prepare a table covered with a cloth upon which the Blessed Sacrament will be placed. A lighted candle(s) is prepared (and, where customary, a container of holy water). A small cross may also be placed on the table, if one is readily available. While this preparation may not be possible in a hospital setting, the administration of communion should not be hurried or habitually mechanical.

c) When the Sunday eucharist is extended to the sick and homebound, communion pyxes are filled after the distribution of communion to the assembly. The ministers of the sick remain near the altar holding their pyxes until after the post-communion prayer. The ministers may then depart in silence or with a brief admonition or blessing (for example, "May the Lord bless you as you carry the gift of the eucharist to our sisters and brothers.").

204.5.3 Policy *The sick who are unable to receive the Holy Eucharist under the form of bread may receive it under the form of wine.*

Procedures

a) The precious blood, consecrated at the most recent Mass and reserved only for this purpose, is carried to the sick in a secure and worthy vessel.

b) Any precious blood that remains after distributing communion to the sick should be consumed by the minister.

c) The vessel is properly purified and is not to be used for any other purpose.

Presiding at Communion Services   §204.6

204.6.1 Policy *Auxiliary ministers of communion at Mass or for the sick may preside at a public communion service provided they have been properly trained and have received the special mandate to preside at these services. (See also §206, Weekday Communion Services, herein.)*

Procedures

a) At the present time the Office for Divine Worship will conduct the archdiocesan training and formation for those who preside at communion services.

b) The Office for Divine Worship will issue a special mandate for these ministers upon completion of their training and formation.

c) Those parishes or institutions desiring to design their own training of lay presiders are to receive prior permission from and consultation with the Office for Divine Worship.

d) Those who have been mandated as auxiliary ministers of communion to the sick may preside at communion services which are celebrated in the homes of the sick and homebound or at the bedside of the infirm without any additional mandate for presiding.

§204.7 Presiding at Exposition of the Blessed Sacrament

204.7.1 Policy *Auxiliary ministers of communion at Mass or to the sick may preside at the exposition of the Blessed Sacrament, provided they have been properly trained and have received the special mandate to preside at these services.*

Procedures

The training of lay presiders for the exposition of the Blessed Sacrament is conducted by the Office for Divine Worship.

204.7.2 Policy *When presiding at the exposition of the Blessed Sacrament, the auxiliary minister shall observe all the ritual prescriptions found in Holy Communion and Worship of the Eucharist Outside of Mass (1976).*

Procedures

a) Lay presiders at the exposition of the Blessed Sacrament do not vest in any special distinctive garb.

b) Lay presiders are not permitted to give the benediction, which is reserved to bishops, priests and deacons.

§205

The Liturgy of the Hours: The Prayer of the Church with Christ and to Christ

Although the revision of the Liturgy of the Hours was completed in 1970, the implementation of the revision of the Mass and the celebration of the sacraments has been the major thrust of our efforts thus far. Now we must consider the promotion of the Liturgy of the Hours as the daily prayer of all God's people.

In the Liturgy of the Hours, the church dedicates both day and night to the Lord's service. It offers thanksgiving and praise and unites work, sufferings and joys to Christ, who prays for us as our priest in his self-offering to the Father (*Catechism of the Catholic Church*, #1174–1178).

While parish communities may not as yet be familiar with or have had much experience with celebrating the Liturgy of the Hours, it is an age-old tradition in the lives of Catholics to pray at the beginning of the day and at the end of the day. In promoting the Liturgy of the Hours, the church is simply building upon that natural Christian movement of the heart and giving form to this personal prayer in union with the whole church. The *General Instruction of the Liturgy of the Hours* states:

> In the Holy Spirit Christ carries out through the church the task of redeeming humanity and giving perfect glory to God, not only when the eucharist is celebrated and the sacraments are administered, but also in other ways and especially when the Liturgy of the Hours is celebrated. There Christ himself is present in the gathered community, in the proclamation of God's word, in the prayer and song of the church (#13).

The Liturgy of the Hours, in which "Christ himself is present," is a rich part of the church's heritage of worship. The availability of its communal celebration should be seriously considered, not only by parishes faced with the lack of a priest for daily eucharist, but by all local assemblies.

By means of thorough education and formation, pastors and pastoral ministers should be encouraged to open to their people the treasures of this liturgy of the church. In those places where daily celebrations of the eucharist may no longer be always available, the Liturgy of the Hours should be considered, not as a poor substitute, but as an integral part of the worship of the church and a splendid part of its heritage.

Since the earliest days of the church's existence, Christians gathered for prayer at certain hours, especially morning and evening. While private prayer is necessary and commendable, community prayer has a special dignity which Jesus himself assigned to it: "Where two or three are gathered in my name, there I am in their midst" (Mt. 18:20).

The purpose of the Liturgy of the Hours is to sanctify the day and all human activity. "The Liturgy of the Hours extends to the different hours of the day the praise and prayer, the memorial of the mysteries of salvation and the foretaste of heavenly glory, which are offered in the eucharistic mystery, 'the center and culmination of the whole life of the Christian community'" (GILH, #12). Hence, both historically and theologically great importance has always been attached to the church's tradition of gathering to pray the Liturgy of the Hours.

Importance of Daily Prayer §205.1

205.1.1 Policy *Parishes shall catechize the faithful about the importance of daily prayer and promote the daily celebration of at least some part of the Liturgy of the Hours.*

Procedures

a) Where the Liturgy of the Hours is celebrated, the basic format outlined in chapter two of the *General Instruction on the Liturgy of the Hours* is to be followed.

b) Parishes are encouraged to consider celebrating one of the hours in conjunction with parish meetings or other gatherings of the faithful, e.g. celebrating night prayer at the conclusion of an evening meeting.

§205.2   Presiding at the Liturgy of the Hours

205.2.1 Policy *Any fully initiated Christian who has been properly trained may preside at the Liturgy of the Hours.*

§205.3   Site of Celebration

205.3.1 Policy *The Liturgy of the Hours may be celebrated in a church, a chapel, or any suitable place.*

§205.4   Music

205.4.1 Policy *Every effort shall be made to incorporate music and a complement of ministers in the celebration of the Liturgy of the Hours.*

§205.5   Incorporation of Distribution of Communion

205.5.1 Policy *While it is permissible to incorporate the distribution of communion into morning or evening prayer, it is not recommended to do so regularly lest the integrity of the Liturgy of the Hours be confused or diminished with this addition.*

§206

Weekday Communion Services

It is to be viewed with sadness that in some parts of the church today a daily Mass is not always possible. Due to the lack of a priest or for other serious reasons, some local assemblies, even on Sundays, are at times unable to celebrate the eucharist. It is in response to this painful situation that the Congregation for Divine Worship has issued the *Directory for Sunday Celebrations in the Absence of a Priest*.

The *Directory for Sunday Celebrations in the Absence of a Priest* was intended to address those situations in which a priest is not able to be present for Sunday Mass. In response to the Roman document, the U.S. National Conference of Catholic Bishops issued its own document, *Gathered in Steadfast Faith*, which provides the rituals that are to be used on those occasions when a communion service is permitted.

In the archdiocese of Chicago we are at this time still fortunate to have a sufficient number of priests to assure regular Sunday celebrations of the Mass in our local communities. Therefore, the implementation of communion services in the absence of a priest on Sunday is not foreseen in the immediate future.[1] However in some places the daily availability of a priest for the celebration of Mass can no longer be presumed. Our response to this situation must be made in the light of the norms articulated in the *Directory for Sunday Celebrations in the Absence of a Priest* and *Gathered in Steadfast Faith*.

When considering the implementation of communion services in the absence of a priest, local communities should be made aware of the limits of this form of liturgy. Neither the presentation of the gifts and the eucharistic prayer, nor the eucharistic actions of taking, giving thanks and breaking the

---

1. See Policies 201.3.1 and 202.11, herein, prohibiting the scheduling of communion services in lieu of Masses on Sunday, Saturday Masses of Anticipation and Holy Day Masses, even when one of the regularly scheduled Masses is canceled.

bread, are found in a communion service. Therefore, communion services do not and cannot accomplish what the Mass intends to do.

Finally, there is a pastoral concern that over a period of time a communion service could come to be perceived as simply "an abbreviated Mass" and an acceptable alternative to the church's traditional eucharistic celebration. Any diminishment in the understanding of the Mass is not acceptable.

The *Directory for Sunday Celebrations in the Absence of a Priest* makes this plain:

> It is imperative that the faithful be taught to see the substitutional character of these celebrations, which should not be regarded as the optimal solution to new difficulties nor as a surrender to mere convenience (#21).

Any confusion between this kind of assembly and a eucharistic celebration must be carefully avoided. Assemblies of this kind should not take away but should rather increase the desire of the faithful to take part in the celebration of the eucharist, and should make them more eager to be present at the celebration of the eucharist (#22).

When celebrating communion services, parishes must constantly attend to their correct implementation and interpretation. Deciding whether and when to offer a communion service is an important pastoral and liturgical decision. The following policies and procedures are offered in the hope of assisting parishes in making these decisions.

It is imperative that the faithful are thoroughly instructed about the meaning and importance of the Sunday eucharist in the life of the church. In addition, the faithful should be taught that the celebration of daily Mass flows from our understanding of the Sunday eucharist.

The following policies and procedures regarding the preparation for celebrating communion services on weekdays are not to be interpreted as advocating communion services as a regular practice. At the same time, we recognize that there are times when daily Mass may not always be available to the faithful. In such limited situations, a communion service may be one of the options considered for daily communal prayer.

Preparing the Parish §206.1

206.1.1 Policy *Pastors, in consultation with the parish council and parish liturgy committee, shall articulate the conditions in the parish when it is considered appropriate to celebrate a communion service. The rationale for these services, based on the introduction to this document and the principles found therein, shall be printed in the parish bulletin with some regularity so that there is no misunderstanding about the difference between the Mass and a communion service. The preeminence of the Mass must be preserved among the faithful.*

206.1.2 Policy *Where communion services are judged to be appropriate, parishes are to be prepared for the possibility that on certain weekdays a communion service, presided over by a deacon or properly trained and mandated lay minister, may be celebrated.*

The Presiding Minister §206.2

Presiders at communion services have the responsibility of leading the complete service: both the liturgy of the word and the giving of holy communion. In addition, other liturgical ministers such as lectors, musicians or servers are to be engaged in communion services as necessary.

206.2.1 Policy *When a priest is not available to preside at Mass, deacons or properly prepared and mandated lay ministers may preside at weekday communion services.*

Procedures

a) Parishes, which determine a need to celebrate communion services, are to send their lay presiders to a training program provided by the

Office for Divine Worship or are to design their own training program in collaboration with the Office for Divine Worship prior to the mandating of these presiders for this ministry.

b) Pastors are to apply to the archbishop through the Office for Divine Worship for a particular mandate of the lay ministers who will preside at communion services. These lay presiders will ordinarily be selected from the parish's auxiliary ministers of communion. If they are not already mandated as an auxiliary minister of communion, they will receive this mandate at the completion of their training.

c) The appointment of lay persons to preside at communion services is to be made known to the parish by means of a liturgical celebration in which prayers are offered to God on behalf of those appointed. The "Order for the Blessing of Those Who Exercise Pastoral Service," contained in the *Book of Blessings*, may be used for this purpose.

d) Lay presiders at communion services may give a reflection on the Scriptures, as long as they have been trained for this purpose and are properly mandated.

e) The presider at a communion service on weekdays should follow the order of service outlined in the *Directory for Sunday Celebrations in the Absence of a Priest* and *Gathered in Steadfast Faith*.

§206.3   Scheduling Communion Services on Weekdays

The situations under which communion services are considered appropriate are limited. Parishes should anticipate these situations by clearly articulating parish policy regarding the scheduling of communion services on weekdays. Moreover, this policy is to be clearly communicated to the community.

206.3.1 Policy *Pastors, in consultation with the parish pastoral council and parish liturgy committee, may schedule a communion service on a weekday whenever there is a genuine pastoral need due to the absence of a priest to celebrate daily Mass. Other options such as the Liturgy of the Hours (without the distribution of holy communion) should be considered first in order to maintain the integrity of communion within its proper context, the Mass.*

206.3.2 Policy *Due to the extraordinary nature of communion services, only one communion service may be scheduled per day in a parish where daily Mass has not been celebrated. Whenever there will be only one daily eucharist, be it a funeral or a wedding, opportunity for community prayer at a regularly scheduled time is encouraged. First consideration is to be given to the Liturgy of the Hours.*

206.3.3 Policy *A communion service may be celebrated at hospitals and nursing homes when a priest is not available to celebrate the eucharist.*

Procedures

When communion is taken to the sick, the ritual to be used is found in *Pastoral Care of the Sick*. This ritual is to be used during visits to the sick at home or in a hospital or nursing home.

Style of Communion Services   §206.4

When communion services are used in a parish, the order of service found in *Gathered in Steadfast Faith* and the *Directory for Sunday Celebrations in the Absence of a Priest* is to be followed.

There ought to be no confusion caused by the manner of the celebration or the way in which the liturgy is announced to the congregation. Any impression that the communion service is a Mass must be avoided.

206.4.1 Policy *Communion services require the same care in preparation and celebration that the church has made normative for all liturgical celebrations. This includes the involvement of other liturgical ministers.*

206.4.2 Policy *Communion is only distributed in the context of the rites that the church provides and shall never be distributed immediately before or after Mass, lest the reception of communion become simply a private devotion disconnected from the Word of God and the prayer of the church.*

Procedures

a) The services provided in *Gathered in Steadfast Faith* are used for weekday celebrations with the following adaptations. On weekdays only one reading is used in addition to the Gospel: The readings are taken from those given in the Lectionary for Mass for weekdays. The opening prayer may be taken from the Sacramentary, especially on feasts or memorials of the saints.

b) The communion rite begins with the Lord's Prayer, which is preceded by the general intercessions. When communion is distributed at morning or evening prayer, the distribution of communion takes place immediately after the gospel canticle. However, morning or evening prayer should not ordinarily include the distribution of communion.

c) Deacons who preside at a communion service act in accord with their ministry with regard to the greetings, the prayers, the gospel reading, the homily, the giving of holy communion, the dismissal, and final blessing. Deacons wear the vestments proper to their ministry, that is, the alb with stole.

d) Lay presiders use those prayers and blessings specifically designated for lay persons.

e) Lay presiders are expected to dress in a dignified manner. They do not wear liturgical vesture (i.e., an alb or stole), lest the communion service be confused with the Mass or the lay presider be mistaken for an ordained minister.

RESOURCES

Preparation

1. Bishops' Committee on the Liturgy. *Study Text II: Eucharistic Worship and Devotion Outside Mass.* Washington: USCC, 1987.
2. Bishops' Committee on the Liturgy. *Gathered in Steadfast Faith: Statement of the Bishops' Committee on the Liturgy on Sunday Worship in the Absence of a Priest.* Washington: USCC, 1990.
3. Bishops' Committee on the Liturgy. *In Spirit and Truth: Black Catholic Reflections on the Order of Mass.* Washington: USCC, 1988.
4. Bishops' Committee on the Liturgy. *Order for Sunday Celebrations in the Absence of a Priest.* Washington: USCC, 1989.
5. Robert Cabie. *The Church at Prayer, Vol. II: The Eucharist.* Collegeville: Liturgical Press, 1986. (See Section V: Worship of the Eucharist Outside Mass, pp. 231–244.)
6. Congregation for Divine Worship. *Directory for Sunday Celebrations in the Absence of a Priest.* Washington: United States Catholic Conference, 1988.
7. Congregation for Divine Worship. *Holy Communion and Worship of the Eucharist Outside of Mass.* Washington: USCC, 1976.
8. Gabe Huck. *The Communion Rite at Sunday Mass.* Chicago: Liturgy Training Publications, 1989.
9. Sacred Congregation of Rites. *General Instruction of the Roman Missal. Liturgy Documentary Series 2.* Washington: USCC, 1982.
10. Sacred Congregation for Divine Worship. *The Liturgy of the Hours: The General Instruction with Commentary,* by A.-M. Roguet. Collegeville: Liturgical Press, 1971.

Presiders

1. Bishops' Committee on the Liturgy. *Order for Sunday Celebrations in the Absence of a Priest.* Washington: USCC, 1989.
2. Charles Gusmer. *Wholesome Worship.* Washington, D.C.: Pastoral Press, 1989.
3. Robert W. Hovda. *Strong, Loving, and Wise: Presiding in Liturgy.* Collegeville: Liturgical Press, 1980.
4. Kathleen Hughes. *Lay Presiding: The Art of Leading Prayer.* Washington: Pastoral Press, 1988.
5. Michael Kwatera. *The Ministry of Communion.* Collegeville: Liturgical Press, 1983.
6. Clare T. Pelkey. *The Body of Christ, A Guide for Eucharistic Ministers.* Notre Dame: Ave Maria Press, 1988.

Scheduling

1. Bishops' Committee on the Liturgy. *Gathered in Steadfast Faith: Statement of the Bishops' Committee on the Liturgy on Sunday Worship in the Absence of a Priest.* Washington: USCC, 1990.
2. Bishops' Committee on the Liturgy. *Order for Sunday Celebrations in the Absence of a Priest.* Washington: USCC, 1989.
3. Congregation for Divine Worship. *Directory for Sunday Celebrations in the Absence of a Priest.* Washington: USCC, 1988.
4. Congregation for Divine Worship. *Holy Communion and Worship of the Eucharist Outside of Mass.* Washington: USCC, 1976.

Auxiliary Ministers

1. *Book of Blessings,* The Roman Ritual, 1989.
2. Canons 230.3 and 910.2.
3. *Fidei Custos.* Instruction on special ministers to administer communion, April 30, 1969. Sacred Congregation for the Discipline of the Sacraments.
4. *General Instruction of the Roman Missal,* 1974.
5. *Holy Communion and Worship of the Eucharist Outside of Mass.* 1973, Sacred Congregation for Divine Worship. ICEL, 1974.
6. Gabe Huck, *The Communion Rite at Sunday Mass.* Chicago: Liturgy Training Publications, 1989.
7. *Immensae Caritatis.* Instruction on facilitating reception of communion in certain circumstances, January 29, 1973. Sacred Congregation for the Discipline of the Sacraments.
8. *Pastoral Care of the Sick.* The Roman Ritual, approved for use in the dioceses of the United States, 1982.
9. *This Holy and Living Sacrifice.* Directory for the Celebration and Reception of Communion Under Both Kinds, NCCB, 1985.

Style

1. Bishops' Committee on the Liturgy. *Gathered in Steadfast Faith: Statement of the Bishops' Committee on the Liturgy on Sunday Worship in the Absence of a Priest.* Washington: USCC, 1990.
2. Bishops' Committee on the Liturgy. *Order for Sunday Celebrations in the Absence of a Priest.* Washington: USCC, 1989.

3. Congregation for Divine Worship. *Directory for Sunday Celebrations in the Absence of a Priest.* Washington: USCC, 1988.

4. Congregation for Divine Worship. *Holy Communion and Worship of the Eucharist Outside of Mass.* Washington: USCC, 1976.

5. Kathleen Hughes. *Lay Presiding: The Art of Leading Prayer.* Washington: Pastoral Press, 1988.

§300

THE SACRAMENT OF PENANCE

■

contents

§300

THE SACRAMENT OF PENANCE

Introduction[1]

"The people of God accomplishes and perfects this continual repentance in many different ways. It shares in the sufferings of Christ by enduring its own difficulties, carries out works of mercy and charity, and adopts ever more fully the outlook of the Gospel message. Thus the people of God becomes in the world a sign of conversion to God. All this the church expresses in its life and celebrates in the liturgy when the faithful confess that they are sinners and ask pardon of God and of their brothers and sisters. This happens in penitential services, in the proclamation of the word of God, in prayer and in the penitential aspects of the eucharistic celebration.

In the sacrament of penance the faithful 'obtain from the mercy of God pardon for their sins against him; at the same time they are reconciled with the church which they wounded by their sins and which works for their conversion by charity, example and prayer.'" (*Rite of Penance*, Introduction, #4)

300.1 Policy *Pastoral practice must follow church teaching and discipline, even though it develops in a specific cultural context. Administration of the sacrament of penance in the archdiocese of Chicago shall be in complete accord with all of the ritual components of the Rite of Penance as promulgated the First Sunday of Advent, 1973.*

Procedures

Particular attention should be given to the Second Vatican Council's *Constitution on the Sacred Liturgy*, to the "Instruction" introducing the Rite of Penance, and to the pertinent canons of the revised *Code of Canon Law* (canons 956–991). This teaching and discipline provide the foundation for the development of an appropriate pastoral practice.

§301

Reconciliation of Individual Penitents (First Form)

Time and Opportunity for Celebration of the Sacrament in this Form   §301.1

301.1.1 Policy *Every parish shall offer ample opportunity to celebrate the sacrament of penance in the individual form.*

Procedures

Various times other than just prior to the Saturday evening Mass should be explored.

301.1.2 Policy *The sacrament of penance shall not be celebrated while a Mass is being celebrated in the same place. (See also Policy 202.12.1, herein.)*

Physical Arrangements   §301.2

301.2.1 Policy *Ordinarily, the Rite for the Reconciliation of Individual Penitents shall be celebrated either in a confessional or a reconciliation room. Confessionals or other suitable arrangements which ensure anonymity of the penitent shall be provided.*

301.2.2 Policy *Every parish church and place of worship must make provision for at least one reconciliation room.*

Procedures

A reconciliation room is, by definition, a physical setting which provides the penitent with all the options of the Rite. It should be of appropriate size and provide a table for the scriptures and a kneeler and screen, as well as a chair for face-to-face confession. Attention should be given to proper lighting, ventilation, acoustics and liturgical symbols. It is not to be used for any purpose other than the celebration of the sacraments.

§301.3 Liturgical Prayer

301.3.1 Policy *The confessional or reconciliation room shall be adjacent to the worship area to make it clear that the sacrament of penance is a liturgical act of worship.*

Procedures

a) So that this form may be clearly understood as an experience of ecclesial and liturgical prayer, the Word of God should be included in the individual form of the sacrament. If the penitent has not prepared for the sacrament by selecting a scripture passage in advance, the confessor may offer a selection either prior to the telling of the sins or later in the rite.

b) The confessor may follow the custom common in the United States of wearing a stole over a cassock or clerical suit. The ideal of alb or surplice and stole, as reflected in the ritual, should not be too easily dismissed.

Assistance in Making a Complete Confession   §301.4

301.4.1 Policy *Church law requires penitents to mention all serious sins, both number and kind, of which they are aware and which have not yet been submitted for individual absolution. Respecting the personal style in which the penitents choose to speak of their sins and discern the movements of the Spirit in their lives, the confessor shall assist them in making a complete confession.*

Procedures

a) The confessor, aware of his own sinfulness and the disorders in human life, may occasionally assist the penitent in identifying the Lord's call to personal growth without unnecessary probing. The confessor should strive to help the penitent in the formation of a Christian conscience and alert him or her to the interior movements of the Holy Spirit.

b) Those with disabilities are to be included in parish celebrations of the sacrament of penance or in celebrations in small communities of faith that are flexible and responsive to a wide range of needs.

   Those with severe limitations can still sense alienation from others and struggle with relationships, love being the first commandment. Unless the celebrant knows the person very well, individual confession may be difficult when there are language problems, affective difficulties, or disorientation relating to time and space.

Penance and Absolution   §301.5

301.5.1 Policy *A penance (also called "Satisfaction") shall be assigned by the priest or mutually agreed upon by confessor and penitent and should be appropriate for the individual.*

Procedures

Even though prayer and self-denial may be more appropriate penance on occasion, an especially appropriate penance could be an exercise in a work of mercy and service to one's neighbor. The penance should be proportionate to the gravity of the sins confessed.

301.5.2 Policy *The church's official words of absolution as found in the Rite of Penance must always be said.*

Procedures

As or after he reflectively prays the words of absolution, the confessor should extend his hands over the penitent whenever physically feasible; if the penitent is behind a screen or in an awkward position for a dignified imposition of hands, the confessor should at least raise his hand toward the penitent.

Those with disabilities are to be included in parish celebrations of the sacrament of penance or in celebrations in small communities of faith that are flexible and responsive to a wide range of needs.

Those with severe limitations can still sense alienation from others and struggle with relationships, love being the first commandment. Unless the celebrant knows the person very well, individual confession may be difficult when there are language problems, affective difficulties, or disorientation relating to time and space.

§302

Reconciliation of Several Penitents with Individual Confession and Absolution (Second Form)

Time and Opportunity for Celebration of the Sacrament in this Form §302.1

302.1.1 Policy *The Rite for Reconciliation of Several Penitents with Individual Confession and Absolution is one of the legitimate options of the Rite of Penance which should be afforded to all the faithful on occasion.*

302.1.2 Policy *This Second Form shall not be used when the numbers present are extremely large (i.e., during Holy Week or the final week before Christmas), thus preventing its proper celebration, or when the participants are not particularly disposed to a communal celebration of this sacrament.*

Physical Arrangements §302.2

302.2.1 Policy *The physical arrangements for celebration of this Second Form shall enable individuals to approach the confessors either face-to-face or anonymously.*

Liturgical Prayer §302.3

302.3.1 Policy *During the communal liturgy, there shall be the usual distribution of liturgical roles.*

Procedures

a) This form of the celebration of the sacrament demands proper and thorough liturgical planning. As with all forms, the basic format of the Rite shall be followed; however, considerable variety is possible in terms of texts, themes, visual and other specific components of the liturgical action.

b) By way of exception, pastoral prudence might occasionally suggest adapting the sacrament so that the service is left open-ended once the individual confessions have begun, i.e., someone concludes the communal prayer after a specified length of time while individual confessions continue to be heard. However, this is a significant departure from what is intended in the Second Form.

c) The Rite of Penance, with its appendices, should be used as a resource book in planning penitential celebrations.

d) Communal prayer and singing are integral components of this form.

e) Additional confessors should be invited to assist in the communal liturgy. Retired members of the presbyterate may be available to assist in these celebrations.

Penance and Absolution §302.4

302.4.1 Policy *When using the Second Form, absolution is always to be given individually to maintain the integrity of the First Form when incorporated into this communal setting.*

---

§303

Reconciliation of Several Penitents with General Confession and General Absolution (Third Form)

Time and Opportunity for Celebration of the Sacrament in this Form   §303.1

303.1.1 Policy *In the archdiocese of Chicago at the present time, there are no generally accepted cases in which the conditions warranting the imparting of general absolution would be foreseen to exist. Should a confessor believe that such conditions exist in individual cases, he is required to obtain prior permission of the diocesan bishop. This policy was enacted by the bishops of the Province of Chicago (November 27, 1988).*

Documentation
The revised Code of Canon Law *specifies the conditions under which general absolution may be imparted. In canon 961, §1, 1°, 2°:*
§1 Absolution cannot be imparted in a general manner to a number of penitents at once without previous individual confession unless:
1° the danger of death is imminent and there is not time for the priest or priests to hear the confessions of the individual penitents;
2° a serious necessity exists, that is, when in light of the number of penitents a supply of confessors is not readily available rightly to hear the confessions of individuals within a suitable time so that the penitents are forced to be deprived of sacramental grace or holy communion for a long time[2] through no fault of their own; it is not considered a sufficient necessity if confessors cannot be readily available only because of the great number of penitents as can occur on the occasion of some great feast or pilgrimage.

§303.2 Liturgical Prayer

303.2.1 Policy *If proper permission is obtained from the diocesan bishop, this Third Form should be celebrated as an integral liturgical action with the usual distribution of liturgical roles.*

303.2.2 Policy *General absolution apart from the setting of such an integral liturgical service is never permitted, except for the situation of immediate danger of death, when absolution alone suffices. It must never be attached as a prelude or appendage to another liturgical service, such as the eucharistic liturgy, a funeral or a wedding.*

§303.3 Penance and Absolution

303.3.1 Policy *For a penitent validly to receive general sacramental absolution, he or she must be suitably disposed and intend in due time to confess serious sins individually. Those participating in the celebration of the Third Form of the sacrament of penance shall be instructed about these obligations and the necessity of making an individual confession of serious sins before again having recourse to general absolution unless a just cause intervenes (canon 963).*

§304

Non-Sacramental Penance Services

304.1 Policy *In addition to three sacramental forms of reconciliation, the Rite of Penance also recommends non-sacramental, communal penance services. These are further options which should be afforded to the faithful several times during the year but particularly during the seasons of Advent and Lent.*

Procedures

The appendices of the Rite of Penance should be used as a resource book in planning such penance services. In planning, publicizing and celebrating such non-sacramental services, the faithful should never be misled into expecting or understanding them as an opportunity for reception of the sacrament.

304.2 Policy *If an ordained minister is not present, a non-ordained minister may preside at such non-sacramental services, thus significantly increasing the opportunities when they may be used.*

Special Pastoral Situations

§305.1   Returning Catholics

305.1.1 Policy *When men and women return to the church after a long absence, seeking to be reconciled, pastoral ministers are to be very sensitive to their personal history and unique spiritual needs. They should be warmly received and shall be given an opportunity to engage in a conversion process that will culminate in the sacrament of penance.*

Procedures

This process may parallel the basic structure of the *Rite of Christian Initiation of Adults* (RCIA).

305.1.2 Policy *Ordinarily, these penitents should not be included in the catechumenate with the unbaptized or with Christians seeking full communion with the church. (See also §107, The Sacrament of Penance and Christian Initiation, herein.)*

§306

Children's Celebration of the Sacrament of Penance[3]

Throughout their catechetical formation, children should be helped to understand the mystery of reconciliation that is at the heart of the church's identity and mission. Within this broader perspective children should be led to understand and appreciate the place of the sacrament of penance in their lives. "Catechesis for children must always respect the natural disposition, ability, age and circumstances of individuals. It seeks, first, to make clear the relationship of the sacrament to the child's life; second, to help the child recognize moral good and evil, repent of wrongdoing and turn to forgiveness to Christ and the church; third, to encourage the child to see that in this sacrament faith is expressed by being forgiven and forgiving; and fourth, to encourage the child to approach the sacrament freely and regularly" (*Sharing the Light of Faith: National Catechetical Directory for Catholics in the United States*, 126).

Preparation for First Reception of the Sacrament of Penance §306.1

306.1.1 Policy *Formal instruction for the sacrament of penance must be separate and distinct from preparation for the first reception of eucharist so that the integrity of each sacrament is maintained.*

Procedures

This formal instruction should begin by the first grade and continue throughout the child's school years. Prior to their first experience of the sacrament of penance, children should communally celebrate throughout the year God's willingness to forgive. It would be well if the child's first experience with the sacrament of penance occurred within a communal setting.

306.1.2 Policy *The parent's right and responsibility to direct the religious formation of their children must be safeguarded and enhanced. For this reason, preparation for first reception of the sacrament shall involve the parents and provide guidance to them in helping prepare their children.*

§306.2 Time and Opportunity for Celebration of the Sacrament of Penance

306.2.1 Policy *Children shall be offered the opportunity to celebrate the sacrament of penance before their first reception of the eucharist (canon 914).*

306.2.2 Policy *The pastor and his staff shall, when necessary, explain to the parents the church's discipline in regard to first confession before first communion and the catechetical reasons for it.*

Procedures

Such an explanation should help the parents understand the values underlying the norm. It is important that both parents and children correctly understand the nature of sin and forgiveness. The sacrament is not intended to be an experience of judgment that condemns but of a love that pardons.

306.2.3 Policy *In those cases in which a child, because of exceptional reasons and under the guidance of his or her parents, chooses not to receive the sacrament of penance, he or she shall not be deprived of the right to receive his or her first communion. The child shall be encouraged to celebrate the Sacrament of Penance later so that he or she will not be deprived of it altogether.*

Physical Arrangements §306.3

306.3.1 Policy *As with adults, children have the right to celebrate the sacrament face-to-face or from behind a screen. Children shall always be free to choose their own confessor.*

RESOURCES

1. Andrew Cuschieri. *The Sacrament of Reconciliation: A Theological and Canonical Treatise.* New York: University Press of America, 1992.
2. James Dallen. *The Reconciling Community: The Rite of Penance.* New York: Pueblo Publishing Company, 1986. Now published by The Liturgical Press.
3. James Dallen & Joseph Favazza, eds. *Removing the Barriers: The Practice of Reconciliation.* Chicago: Liturgy Training Publications, 1991.
4. Martin Doodle & Geoffrey Rowell, eds. *Confession and Absolution.* Collegeville: Liturgical Press, 1990.
5. Timothy E. O'Connell. *Principles for a Catholic Morality,* revised edition. San Francisco: Harper & row, 1990.
6. Robert J. Kennedy, ed. *Reconciliation: The Continuing Agenda.* Collegeville: Liturgical Press, 1987.
7. *Rite of Penance.* Catholic Books Publishing Co., New York. 1975.
8. Province of Chicago. *The Sacrament of Penace: Guidelines for the Dioceses of Illinois* (November 27, 1988).
9. Jeffrey Sobosan. *Act of Contrition: Personal Responsibility and Sin.* Notre Dame: Ave Maria Press, 1979.
10. Xavier Thevenot. *Sin: A Christian View for Today.* Liguori: Liguori Publications, 1984.

ENDNOTES

1. For celebration of the sacrament of penance in conjunction with the process of initiation, see §107, herein.
2. The National Conference of Catholic Bishops has determined that the word *diu* ("for a long time") in Canon 961, §1,2° should be understood as "a month."
3. See also Policy 107.3.1 concerning the celebration of the sacrament of penance for non-Catholic children seeking formal reception into the Catholic church.

§400

THE SACRAMENT OF MARRIAGE

■

contents

§400

THE SACRAMENT OF MARRIAGE

§404 Style of Marriage Celebrations

Resources

Introduction

What a wonderful gift it is for a parish community to celebrate the love of a man and woman in the sacrament of matrimony! In witnessing this love the community is reminded of the love of Christ for his bride, the church (Ephesians 5:22).

In ministering to the engaged couple and in celebrating their marriage, the church not only expresses its love and support for the couple but acknowledges the value of their married life as a help to each other to attain holiness and as a blessing for society and the life of the church. In forming a family, they become a domestic church. By word and example they are the first heralds of the faith with regard to their children (*Dogmatic Constitution on the Church*, #11).

In his pastoral letter on the church, *The Family Gathered Here Before You*, Joseph Cardinal Bernardin affirms the importance of family life in helping people live a life a faith:

> The "domestic church," whatever its particular shape, contains in a very simple form many of the essential ingredients of ecclesial life in the Catholic tradition: proclamation of God's Word, sacramental life, works of service, forgiveness and reconciliation, worship, and the impetus to mission in and to the world. It leads its members naturally to live the fullness of ecclesial life in the larger community of the church.

Because of the seriousness of the vocation of Christian marriage, the church has an obligation to do all that it can to preserve the dignity of marriage and offer its members the guidance and support that will help to prepare a couple for their married life.

Parish ministers sometimes encounter couples for whom the beautiful and exalted image of marriage as a sacrament seems far from their experience. These couples may not worship regularly or be fully catechized. They may have drifted away from actively practicing their faith in high school or college. Their notions of marriage may be more influenced by television and the movies than by the Christian tradition. One of the partners may not be a Catholic or a Christian. This is undoubtedly a challenge to pastoral ministers.

It is not a rare pastoral experience to meet a couple for whom the marriage preparation is their first experience as adults of encountering the church. They may come with fear or apprehension. They may come with misconceptions or unreasonable expectations. But their coming to the church at this important time in their lives is in itself a movement of grace.

Pastoral ministers need to see in these occasions an opportunity for evangelization. A warm welcome and a genuine concern for their welfare may be a turning point in their lives as they experience the church from a new perspective. This demands patience, sensitivity, and above all, a love that can both challenge as well as rejoice with the couple preparing for marriage.

These policies and procedures cannot cover every possible situation pastoral ministers will encounter in serving the needs of the engaged. However, they are intended to give order and direction to our celebration of marriage in the archdiocese of Chicago.

While respecting the personal and familial nature of each marriage celebration, the church has an obligation in the exercise of its teaching office to lead and guide all the faithful to a truly Catholic understanding of marriage as a public act, a communal treasure, a sacrament of the church.

Through homilies, special programs and all forms of catechesis, those entrusted with pastoral responsibility must continually strive to help the faithful to achieve the ideals of Christian marriage (*Catechism of the Catholic Church*, #1601 – 1666).

§401

Preparation for Christian Marriage

The vocation of Christian marriage demands a serious commitment. Consequently, the church desires to do all that it can so that couples be adequately prepared to accept the obligations of Christian marriage and to fulfill them faithfully.

§401.1 A Lifetime Commitment

401.1 Policy *The parish community shall take responsibility for preparing couples not only for their wedding day but for the lifetime commitment of living a Christian marriage.*

§401.2 Minimum of Four Months of Preparation

401.2.1 Policy *The formal preparation for marriage shall begin at least four months before the anticipated date of the wedding.*

§401.3 Setting the Wedding Date

401.3.1 Policy *No firm date for a wedding shall be set until the conclusion of the couple's first meeting with the parish minister.*

401.3.2 Policy *If during the couple's meeting with the parish minister, the minister determines there was a previous marriage, no firm or even tentative wedding date shall be entered in the parish calendar until freedom to marry has been established through appropriate canonical procedures and documentation.*

Marriage Preparation Programs §401.4

401.4.1 Policy *In addition to personal interviews, instruction and counseling from the parish staff, the archdiocese of Chicago offers a variety of marriage preparation programs to meet the individual needs of engaged couples. The parish minister shall recommend the appropriate marriage preparation program in which the couple is to participate.*

Procedures

a) Priests, deacons, and pastoral associates are to share the responsibility for preparing couples for marriage with parishioners who have received suitable catechesis and training in marriage preparation and who can appropriately minister to engaged couples.

b) It is strongly urged that there be six sessions devoted to marriage preparation:

- Session I: Initial meeting with parish minister
- Sessions II, III, and IV may be satisfied by three sessions with a pastoral minister or by attending a marriage preparation program:

  - PreCana
  - Special PreCana
  - PreCana II
  - PreCana Hispana
  - Hispanic PreCana in English
  - PreCana Hispana Especial
  - PreCana for the African-American community
  - Italian PreCana
  - Polish PreCana
  - Discovery Weekend
  - Parish Marriage Preparation Program

- Session V: Follow-up session with parish minister
- Session VI: Follow-up session with parish minister

c) Expectations for marriage preparation are to appear in the parish bulletin and in parish sacramental handbooks.

§401.5 Delaying the Wedding

401.5.1 Policy *When special circumstances are present (i.e., an unwillingness to prepare for marriage, a lack of openness to faith, a serious lack of maturity, teenagers 18 years of age or younger, pregnancy, extended separation before or after the wedding) or if some reasonable question is raised concerning the couple's readiness to marry, further consultation and evaluation are required before a wedding date can be set.*

To insure that a couple's rights are respected, a couple must be informed of their right to appeal the decision to delay their wedding date to the Office of the Chancellor (312-751-8207).

Procedures

a) The parish minister should consult with the Office of the Chancellor.

b) Upon consultation with a representative of the Office of the Chancellor, the parish minister can decide:

    1. The special circumstances are not of a serious enough nature to impede a couple's ability to enter into a successful marriage. When such a decision is reached, the date of the wedding can be set and formal marriage preparation can begin.

    2. Additional information is needed. The parish minister will undertake a more in-depth assessment. No date for the wedding can be set until a positive decision has been made.

§402

The Presiding Minister and Witnesses for the Rite of Marriage

The celebration of Catholic marriage takes place in the midst of the community. The presiding minister, who is the official witness of marriage for the church, is presumed to have a pastoral relationship with the couple.

Responsibility for Witnessing §402.1

402.1.1 Policy *Priests and deacons who have appropriate faculties have the responsibility for witnessing Catholic marriages.*

Procedures

a) Presbyteral faculties of the archdiocese provide that all priests incardinated in the archdiocese of Chicago have the faculty to witness all marriages within the archdiocese when one party is of the Latin rite. For liceity, this faculty is to be exercised only with the consent of the local pastor or his delegate. (See Faculties 805.1 and 805.2.)

Religious order priests or externs who are assigned as territorial pastors or associate pastors have the faculty to assist validly at marriages within their boundaries for parishioners or for non-parishioners provided one is of the Latin rite. For liceity, permission of the proper pastor is required.

Religious order priests or externs who are pastors or associate pastors of non-territorial parishes can assist validly only at marriages within the limits of their jurisdiction involving at least one of their own parishioners.

Visiting priests who have faculties to witness marriages in their dioceses may obtain faculties to witness a marriage in the archdiocese of Chicago from the local pastor of the parish in which the marriage is to take place or from the chancery (canon 1111).

Diaconal faculties of the archdiocese provide that permanent deacons, incardinated in the archdiocese and having completed the certification program in marriage preparation, are granted the faculty to assist validly at all marriages within the archdiocese when one party is of the Latin rite. If the local parish does not have a copy of the deacon's certification on file, the local pastor should contact the vicar for the diaconate community for verification and a copy of the certification. For liceity, this faculty is to be exercised only with the consent of the local pastor or his delegate. Deacons who have not received this general grant of delegation need to obtain special delegation for each marriage from the local pastor or his delegate.

b) The responsibility for celebrating marriage outside of Mass is not the sole responsibility of deacons. Priests and deacons share this responsibility.

c) When deacons minister at a marriage celebrated at Mass, the priest who presides at the Mass is ordinarily the witness of the marriage vows. For pastoral reasons, exceptions may be allowed to permit the deacon to witness the marriage vows at Mass.

d) Transitional deacons may witness a Catholic marriage only with the proper delegation of the ordinary. This delegation may be obtained through the Office of the Chancellor.

e) For weddings that would involve a non-Catholic officiant, consult the Province of Chicago Ecumenical Guidelines (1986).

§402.2   Special Language and Cultural Needs

402.2.1 Policy *Parishes shall provide a Catholic minister who can attend to the special language and cultural needs of those being married in the churches of the archdiocese of Chicago.*

Procedures

a) In a parish where the local ministers cannot meet the special language or cultural needs of their parishioners, the parish staff is to seek the assistance of other Catholic clergy who can minister to engaged couples with special needs. This presumes that these Catholic clergy will also participate in the marriage preparation of those whose marriages they witness.

b) When parishes can find no ordained clergy available to meet the special language or cultural needs of their people, they are to contact the Office of the Chancellor or the Ethnic Ministries Office to inquire about the possibility of making special arrangements for the particular individuals.

c) When the special language or cultural needs involve Catholics of an Eastern Catholic church, see §404.6, Latin Rite and Eastern Rite/ Eastern Catholic Weddings.

d) In the foreseeable future it does not appear that the number of clergy will be so limited that the archdiocese will have to seek an indult from Rome allowing a lay person to witness marriages in the archdiocese.

Non-Catholic Witnesses §402.3

402.3.1 Policy *Although it is preferable that both witnesses at a marriage ceremony in the Catholic church be Catholic, when circumstances warrant, one or both may be other than Catholic without the need for special permission from the Chancery. It should be noted that if there are other attendants in addition to the best man and maid/matron of honor, any two Catholics among them may be designated as the official witnesses (Statement on the Implementation of the Apostolic Letter on Mixed Marriages, NCCB, January 1, 1971, p. 14, n. 58).*

§402.4   Catholics as Witnesses at Non-Catholic Weddings

402.4.1 Policy *Catholics may serve as witnesses at weddings of friends of other faiths except where there is reason to believe that the marriage to be witnessed is invalid (Interdiocesan Program for Ecumenism, 1971, p. 33).*

§403

Establishing Marriage Celebration Schedules

A fair and reasonable parish policy needs to be established to ensure that Catholics have reasonable options available to them in scheduling their marriages at Mass or outside Mass. This will have to take into account the full schedule of parish services and the number of available clergy in each parish.

The parish policy for the scheduling of marriage celebrations should be clearly communicated to all parishioners. The parish policy should appear regularly in the parish bulletin and be available in print as part of whatever marriage preparation materials are given to engaged couples.

Since the number of weddings celebrated at Mass may be limited in a particular parish, couples should be helped to understand that it will not always be possible to celebrate a wedding on the day of their first choice. (See §202, Mass Schedules, herein.)

In the scheduling of marriage liturgies, the communal nature of the sacrament of marriage should be fostered. Appropriate catechesis of the faithful is necessary to help the community to understand the communal dimension of this sacrament. This is especially important if marriages are to be celebrated occasionally at a regularly scheduled Sunday Mass or if several marriages are celebrated together.

In establishing a parish marriage schedule, the integrity of the liturgical calendar and the community's celebration of Sunday should be respected.

§403.1   Parish's Restriction of Number of Weddings

403.1.1 Policy *A parish, through consultation with the parish pastoral council and the liturgy committee, may develop a policy restricting the number of weddings on a given day depending on the pastoral situation and the number of ministers available to celebrate marriages. This parish policy also includes the scheduling of special wedding anniversary Masses.*

Procedures

a) church law (canon 905) expressly prohibits priests celebrating more than one Mass a day except in those cases where the law permits multiple celebrations. This law allows the ordinary to permit a priest to celebrate two Masses on a weekday and three Masses on a Sunday or Holy Day. The ordinary does not have the authority to authorize more Masses to be celebrated by an individual priest.

b) If a parish has a large number of weddings, after reviewing the weekend parish Mass schedule in consultation with the parish pastoral council and the liturgy committee, it is possible to eliminate the Saturday morning Mass. (See Policies 202.9 and 202.10, herein.)

c) When the Mass in which the sacrament of marriage is celebrated is a regular parish Sunday Mass, the Mass of the day is celebrated.

d) On a Sunday in Ordinary Time, when a wedding is celebrated at a regularly scheduled parish Mass, one of the readings may be chosen from those provided in the Lectionary for ritual masses for weddings.

e) Weddings on solemnities such as All Souls Day are permitted, but the texts of the Mass are those of the solemnity.

f) If a wedding Mass is celebrated on Sunday outside the regular Sunday Mass schedule, the selection of liturgical texts is as follows:

- On Sundays of the Christmas Season and throughout the year, the text of the wedding Mass may be used without change;
- On Sundays of Advent, Lent and Easter, the wedding Mass may not be used, but one of the readings of the Ritual (nos. 67–105) should be used;
- On feasts of Christmas, Epiphany, Ascension, Pentecost, Corpus Christi, Assumption, All Saints, Immaculate Conception,

and Mary, Mother of God (Jan. 1), the Mass of the day is used without change except for the nuptial blessings and, where appropriate, the special final blessing (see the *Rite of Marriage*, # 11). Weddings are not permitted during the Paschal Triduum.

g) Since the precept of participating in the Mass is satisfied by assistance at a Mass that is celebrated anywhere in a Catholic rite, either on the Holy Day or on the evening of the preceding day, a Catholic satisfies the obligation by attending any mass, including wedding Masses, on a Sunday, Holy Day, Saturday evening or the vigil of a Holy Day (c. 1248). While the *Code of Canon Law* does not provide an explicit definition, "evening" is generally understood as late afternoon from about 4:00 PM.

More Than One Wedding at Same Ceremony §403.2

403.2.1 Policy *Parish communities may invite more than one couple to consider celebrating their weddings at the same ceremony or Mass. Parishes shall continue to offer couples the option, however, of having individual celebrations of marriage (canon 1115).*

Celebration at Saturday Evening Mass of Anticipation §403.3

403.3.1 Policy *Weddings may be celebrated at a Saturday evening Mass of anticipation, but this should ordinarily not take place more than once a month. The Sunday liturgy is to be celebrated as provided in the* General Norms for the Liturgical Year and the Calendar.

§403.4 Visiting Clergy

403.4.1 Policy *If visiting Catholic clergy have been invited to witness a wedding, it is understood that they are to honor the parish's scheduling policy as well as archdiocesan and parochial expectations for marriage preparation and the celebration of the liturgy.*

§404

Style of Marriage Celebrations

The Catholic experience of celebrating marriage vows clearly conveys the church's beliefs about the sacrament of marriage. The *Rite of Marriage* needs to be respected in its structure and content.

The pastoral circumstances of the couples' religious and family background and practice, language and culture, the available resources of the parish, liturgical norms and canon law are all to be considered in the course of planning the celebration of Christian marriage. The *Rite of Marriage* offers a number of legitimate options to meet these various needs.

Clergy and laity involved in the marriage preparation of engaged couples should help couples appreciate the liturgical nature and the liturgical norms relevant to the *Rite of Marriage*. Parish ministers should encourage engaged couples to avoid all forms of extravagance that would detract from the sacred character of marriage as a sacrament of the church.

The *Rite of Marriage* for two Catholics may take place at Mass. However, this presumes that the couple regularly participate in the Sunday eucharist and are not strangers to their own faith tradition. In some cases, pastoral ministers may need to respectfully encourage the celebration of marriage outside of Mass.

Parish policies governing the style of marriage celebrations in the parish should be clearly communicated to and available in print for engaged couples. These parish policies should appear at regular intervals in the parish bulletin.

Because there are a number of canonical and legal consequences to a marriage celebrated in church, it is important for the parish priest or deacon to process all the necessary documentation required by civil law and the canon law of the church. Accurate records and adherence to requirements for particular documentation, including dispensations, where applicable, are a serious pastoral responsibility. When a visiting priest is delegated to witness a marriage, the parish priest is responsible for seeing that all necessary documentation has been procured prior to the wedding.

§404.1　Restrictions on Priest Officiating

404.1.1 Policy *In the* Rite of Marriage, *the presiding minister serves as the church's official witness. A priest is never permitted to officiate at a wedding in the role of merely a civil official; nor may he officiate at a wedding in which neither of the parties is Catholic, except in the case of catechumens. (See §106.1, Christian Marriages Involving Catechumens, herein)*

Procedures

Concelebration at marriage liturgies is ordinarily to be avoided, since concelebration is a sign of the unity of the priesthood and not a means of adding more solemnity to the liturgy. Only at the invitation of the bride and groom is a priest to consider concelebrating at a nuptial Mass.

§404.2　Assembly Participation

404.2.1 Policy *As is the norm in all liturgical celebrations, the assembly shall be encouraged to participate in the wedding liturgy by making the proper recited and sung responses.*

§404.3　Place of Wedding

404.3.1 Policy *Marriages ordinarily shall take place in a parish church.*

Procedures

a) For students or employees of Northwestern University, the University of Chicago or the University of Illinois at Chicago, or for those who have graduated within the past six months from these universities, marriages may be celebrated in Sheil Chapel, Bond Chapel or Rockefeller Chapel, or the John Paul II Center, respectively.

b) With a dispensation from canonical form, a marriage may take place in a non-Catholic place of worship.

c) In the case of a Catholic-Jewish wedding, the custom of having the marriage in a hotel or place of reception may be followed with the usual dispensations from canonical form and disparity of cult.

404.3.2 Policy *All Catholics who are baptized and free to marry in the Catholic church may celebrate their marriages in the parish church of either the bride or the groom. Permission to be married in another parish is to be obtained from the pastor either of the bride or of the groom.*

Celebrating Marriage Outside of Mass §404.4

404.4.1 Policy *In a marriage between a Catholic and a baptized non-Catholic, it is expected that the Rite for Celebrating Marriage Outside Mass be used. The eucharist is a symbol of Christian unity. Celebrating Christian marriage at Mass may make the celebration awkward for both parties by highlighting their differences in faith. This awkwardness is further accentuated in cases where non-Catholic clergy are invited to participate in a marriage celebrated at Mass.*

If circumstances justify it and the non-Catholic party agrees to having a Mass, "the rite for celebrating marriage within Mass may be used, except that, according to the general law, communion is not given to the non-Catholics." (See Province of Chicago Ecumenical Guidelines, # 111.)

404.4.2 Policy *In the archdiocese of Chicago, the distribution of Holy Communion shall not be included in marriage ceremonies celebrated outside of Mass. While the* Rite of Marriage *allows a communion service to be celebrated after the wedding ceremony, a sufficient number of priests available to celebrate a wedding Mass in the archdiocese of Chicago makes the use of this option unnecessary in the archdiocese.*

The only exception to this policy is when a deacon presides at a wedding ceremony in order to meet the special language or cultural needs of a couple. In such an instance, a communion service, while not encouraged, is permitted.

§404.5 Ecumenical Courtesy

404.5.1 Policy *When planning a marriage between a Catholic and a baptized non-Catholic, the norms of ecumenical courtesy shall be observed.*

Procedures

a) *The Norm of Reciprocity:* As a general rule one should neither extend nor accept an invitation to participate in an ecumenical or interfaith activity unless one may extend or accept a similar invitation in return.

b) *The Norm of Collaboration:* When planning any ecumenical or interfaith activity or service, there should be consultation and collaboration of representatives of all the participating faiths or communions from the beginning. (See *Province of Chicago Ecumenical Guidelines,* chapter 5: *Worship Services.*)

c) Clergy and laity are to make every effort to implement the procedures and norms set forth in the *Province of Chicago Ecumenical Guidelines* for dealing with Eastern non-Catholics. (See chapter 6, *The Sacraments and Eastern non-Catholics.*)

d) Parish ministers who have questions regarding an inter-ritual marriage should seek the counsel of the Office of Ecumenism and Interreligious Affairs or the Office of the Chancellor.

Latin Rite/Eastern Catholic Weddings §404.6

404.6.1 Policy *Marriages between Catholics of the Latin rite and Catholics of an Eastern Catholic church shall take place in the church of either the bride or groom as long as the presider is a minister of one of the churches. Permission of both the proper pastor and the Office of the Chancellor is required to have the marriage celebrated elsewhere (canon 1109).*

404.6.2 Policy *For validity, the officiating priest in a marriage between a Catholic of the Latin rite and a Catholic of an Eastern church must be of the same rite as that of one of the parties.*

Procedures

There are special regulations which must be followed carefully for marriages between Catholics of the Latin Rite and Catholics of Eastern churches. All questions regarding such marriages are to be addressed to the Office of the Chancellor.

It is advisable to consult with the Office of the Chancellor on all interritual cases.

Catholic/Eastern Non-Catholic Weddings §404.7

404.7.1 Policy *When a marriage is celebrated between a Catholic and a non-Catholic, only one religious ceremony is to take place. If the marriage is celebrated in the Catholic church, the Roman Catholic ritual is used and, for the sake of integrity, the rituals of the two traditions should not be integrated into one ceremony.*

Procedures

a) The *Province of Chicago Ecumenical Guidelines*, # 60 provides for the following exception: In a marriage between a Catholic party and an Eastern non-Catholic, the canonical form obliges only for lawfulness; for validity, however, the presence of a sacred minister is required with the observance of the other requirements of law. While two ceremonies are not ideal, some exceptional situations involving Orthodox Christians could call for a special blessing of the marriage. So long as the vows are not repeated, this could be permitted.

b) Christian marriages entered by an Eastern non-Catholic and another non-Catholic before someone other than an Eastern non-Catholic priest are considered invalid by the Catholic church, and a declaration of nullity for such marriages can be obtained from the Chancery in a procedure similar to Catholic Defect of Form cases.

c) Marriages between Latin rite Catholics and Eastern non-Catholic Christians entered without a dispensation from canonical form on or after March 24, 1967, before an Eastern non-Catholic priest are considered valid; such marriages between Eastern Catholics and Eastern non-Catholic Christians entered on or after January 21, 1965 (April 7, 1965 for Ukrainian Catholics) are also considered valid.

§404.8 Marriage Ceremonies Involving Non-Christians and Catechumens

404.8.1 Policy *Marriages involving a non-Christian (after reception of a dispensation from disparity of cult), shall be celebrated at a liturgy of the word and not at the eucharistic liturgy. (See the* Rite of Marriage, *# 8.) While recognizing that catechumens are already joined to the household of the church, marriages involving catechumens shall likewise be celebrated at a liturgy of the word. Chapter III of the* Rite of Marriage *is to be followed with allowance for the nuptial blessing in Chapter I, # 33, to be used (omitting all references to eucharistic sharing). (See National Statutes for the Catechumenate, # 10, and §100, The Sacraments of Initiation, Policy 106.4, herein.)*

Catholic/Jewish Weddings §404.9

404.9.1 Policy *A Catholic priest or deacon with the faculty to witness marriages may witness the marriage of a Catholic/Jewish couple with the usual dispensation from disparity of cult. The preferred choice would be to celebrate the marriage in the Catholic church or in a chapel or other suitable place on parish property. The Catholic marriage ritual for a wedding between a Catholic and an unbaptized person is used.*

Procedures

a) The Jewish rabbi can be invited to participate in the ceremony, but the Catholic priest or deacon officially witnesses the exchange of vows. (See Policy 404.3, herein.)

b) In all of the above situations, Catholic priests and deacons should be aware of the sensitive nature of ministering to a Catholic-Jewish engaged couple. Pastoral care prior to and following the wedding should offer the couple support and assistance. Priests and deacons should not hesitate to get involved in these situations and participate in the marriage ceremony.

(Also see §404.3, Place of Wedding, herein.)

Catholic/Muslim Weddings §404.10

404.10.1 Policy *A Catholic priest or deacon with the faculty to witness marriages may witness the marriage of a Catholic/Muslim couple with the usual dispensation from disparity of cult. Because the situations of these couples are very diverse and complex, the pastoral care before marriage must follow a different process from the usual process in mixed marriages. All preparation for Catholic/Muslim marriages should be planned in consultation with the Office of Ecumenical and Interreligious Affairs.*

Procedures

A Catholic Rite of Marriage is preferred, modified to include sensitivity to the Muslim party.

> **Special Note:** *There is no traditional Islamic marriage rite other than the witnessing of the contract and the public transfer of the bride to the house of the groom. Given that this traditional form can include elements foreign to Christian marriage, very careful planning and agreement must precede any dispensation to allow this rite. For example, the traditional form usually requires the partner to make the profession of faith which converts a person to Islam as a prior condition. Since this would constitute apostasy by formal act, it is impossible for the Catholic to participate in such a ritual. It is conceivable, though, that with careful consultation a modified traditional Islamic celebration could be planned which would be acceptable, and a dispensation could be granted for this form.*

§404.11 Catholic/Non-Monotheist Weddings

404.11.1 Policy *A Catholic priest or deacon with the faculty to witness marriages may witness the marriage of a Catholic to a follower of a non-monotheistic religion (some of the Asian religions, Buddhism, Hinduism, etc.) with a dispensation from disparity of cult. The Office of Ecumenism and Interreligious Affairs may be consulted in planning those marriages.*

Procedures

The Catholic Rite of Marriage is preferred, modified to include sensitivity to the non-Christian party.

> **Special Note:** *The traditional wedding ceremonies in some other religions include rites which in effect would constitute joining another religion (communicatio in sacris). For this reason a pastoral minister should inquire carefully into the religious significance of traditional wedding customs before permitting them to be included in a Catholic ceremony. This becomes all the more important if a Catholic wishes a dispensation to marry in a non-monotheistic religion's ceremony. In some cases, the dispensation may not be possible.*

Respecting Liturgical Roles of Participants §404.12

404.12.1 Policy *The wedding couple shall be helped to appreciate their special role in the marriage rite in which they confer the sacrament on one another through the exchange of vows. Respecting the principle that only one role should be exercised at the liturgy by each individual, other members of the family and parish community, depending on their gifts, shall be invited to participate in the marriage liturgy as lectors, cantors, musicians or ushers. Mandated auxiliary ministers of Holy Communion can be invited to assist in the distribution of Holy Communion, if needed.*

404.12.2 Policy *It is inappropriate for the wedding couple to administer Holy Communion to each other or to the assembly. Their role in the marriage rite is to exchange vows, not to assist the priest in distributing communion. It is also inappropriate for the wedding couple to stand on either side of the presider during the eucharistic prayer as if they were concelebrants.*

Admission of Non-Catholic Persons to Holy Communion §404.13

404.13.1 Policy *Admission to Holy Communion at a Catholic wedding is not possible under present circumstances for members of non-Catholic churches. Specific norms governing admission are clearly articulated in the* Province of Chicago Ecumenical Guidelines *(chapter six for Orthodox Christians and chapter seven for Anglican and Protestant Christians).*

§404.14 Integration of Ethnic and Folk Customs

404.14.1 Policy *Ethnic and folk customs associated with the celebration of marriage in the Catholic church in other countries are to be respected and may be incorporated into the liturgy. The manner in which these or any other customs are incorporated into the liturgy must always respect the integrity of the liturgy and the universal principles articulated in the* Rite of Marriage.

Procedures

When questions arise regarding the appropriateness of a proposed cultural adaptation of the rite of Christian marriage, parishes are to consult with the Office for Divine Worship.

§404.15 Selection of Music

404.15.1 Policy *The selection of music for the wedding liturgy is often a sensitive issue for couples, parish musicians and parish staff. The choice of music at weddings must be in accord with all the norms governing music in the liturgy, especially those found in* Liturgical Music Today *and* Music in Catholic Worship.

Procedures

a) Sometimes the only music familiar to the couple is a song heard at a friend's wedding ceremony and not one necessarily suitable to the sacrament. The pastoral musician will make an effort to demonstrate a wider range of possibilities to the couple, particularly in the choice of music to be sung by the entire assembly present for the liturgy (*Liturgical Music Today, #*28).

b) Particular decisions about choice and placement of wedding music should grow out of the three judgments proposed in *Music in Catholic*

Worship: "The liturgical judgment: Is the music's text, form, placement, and style congruent with the nature of liturgy? The musical judgment: Is the music technically, aesthetically and expressively good, irrespective of musical idiom or style? The pastoral judgment: Will it help this assembly to pray?" (*Liturgical Music Today, #* 29.)

c) Popular love songs that were composed for entertainment rather than liturgical purposes are not ordinarily congruent with the nature of liturgy. Hence, they should be avoided during the liturgical celebration.

Responsibility for Necessary Documentation

§404.16

404.16.1 Policy *The parish priest or deacon arranging the marriage celebration is responsible for obtaining all necessary documentation and processing all forms required by the* Code of Canon Law.

Procedures

a) A baptismal certificate issued within the last six months should always be obtained.

b) Baptismal certificates should always be authenticated personally by one of the priests, deacons or parish ministers. They should always include a statement about the presence or absence of a notation about a previous marriage, religious profession or ordination.

c) Photocopies of documents (i.e., baptismal and marriage certificates, divorce papers, etc.) should not be accepted unless they are certified by a priest or proper authority.

d) Permission for mixed religion may be granted by any priest who is in good standing and is incardinated in the archdiocese or has been approved by the archbishop to minister within the archdiocese. (See Faculty 805.5)

e) The civil requirements for marriage (e.g. a civil marriage license) must be met prior to the celebration of marriage in the church.

f) Requests for dispensations for disparity of cult and special permissions should be accompanied by the full premarital file. This includes the prenuptial questionnaire, recent baptismal records, all legal documents (civil or ecclesiastical) needed to confirm the parties' freedom to marry, and witness affidavits if needed. Dispensation forms should be filled out fully and the names of the parties should be entered on the return stub.

g) If a decree of nullity of the previous marriage has been issued by the Tribunal, a copy of this should be included in the papers submitted to the Chancery for a *Nihil Obstat*. If the decree places a restriction of any kind on the party planning to enter a new marriage, no wedding date should be set before first contacting the Chancery for additional information and consultation (canon 1684.1).

h) Petitions for a declaration of nullity due to lack of form must be filled out fully and signed by both the petitioner and the parish minister. Such petitions must be accompanied by the following documents: a certificate of the marriage attempted outside the church, a record of the civil divorce or annulment, a recent baptismal certificate of the Catholic party, and affidavits from two qualified witnesses testifying that the marriage in question was never validated by a Catholic priest or deacon. No wedding date should be set for a marriage requiring a declaration of nullity due to lack of form until after the decree of nullity has been issued.

i) Requests for prenuptial permissions, dispensations or a *Nihil Obstat*, as well as for declarations of nullity due to lack of form, should be sent to the Chancery. The Matrimonial Tribunal handles only formal and documentary annulment processes and all Pauline Privilege and Privilege of the Faith cases.

j) Dispensations from canonical form can be granted only by the local ordinary of the Catholic party and not by the ordinary of the place where the marriage will be celebrated. Prenuptial papers for a marriage celebrated with a dispensation from canonical form are to be filed in the parish that made application.

k) According to traditional protocol, marriage papers for marriages to be celebrated in a Catholic church in another diocese should be transmitted through the Office of the Chancellor to the diocese where the marriage will be celebrated.

l) A *Nihil Obstat* is to be obtained from the Chancery Office for the convalidation of civil marriages performed by a non-Catholic minister, a rabbi or a civil authority.

m) No fee is required for marriage permissions, dispensations or declarations of nullity due to lack of form.

n) Marriages are to be recorded according to the proper procedures in the parish record book of marriages. Notification of the marriage is sent to the church of Baptism. (See §902.4, Marriage Registers.)

Wedding Offerings

404.17.1 Policy *The Bishops of the Province of Chicago have established a limit of $500.00 as the suggested offering for weddings, exclusive of other expenses (i.e., musicians). (See §203.3, Offerings for Weddings and Funerals, herein.)*

§404.17

Special Note: *The Christian vocation to the married state only begins with the celebration of the nuptial liturgy. The church desires that Christian couples be given ample support and opportunities to grow and mature in the bond of love that is sealed before God and the community. Every parish is encouraged to provide a ministry to those who are married. Ongoing enrichment for the married couple and support for their family life as a sacred and valuable gift to the church needs to be evident in parish life.*

RESOURCES

Preparation

1. Cana Office. *Cana Conference Marriage Preparation Brochure.* Annual calendar of programs in the archdiocese of Chicago.
2. Cana Office. *A Ministry to Marriage.* Chicago, 1985.
3. Austin Fleming. *Parish Weddings.* Chicago: Liturgy Training Publications, 1987.
4. "A Marriage in the Lord," Cana Office, 1991.
5. "Un Matrimonio en el Señor," Cana Office, 1986.
6. *Pastoral Guidelines for Marriage Preparation in the Archdiocese of Chicago,* revised edition. 1991.
7. *The Rite of Marriage,* nos. 5 and 7.

Presiders

1. *The Code of Canon Law,* Canons 905, 1108 and 1111.
2. Michael Kwatera. *The Liturgical Ministry of Deacons.* Collegeville: The Liturgical Press, 1985, pp. 63 – 66.
3. *Province of Chicago Ecumenical Guidelines,* 1986, nos. 95 – 115.
4. *The Rite of Marriage,* nos. 6, 8, and 9.
5. United States Catholic Conference Department of Education. *Faith and Culture: A Multicultural Catechetical Resource.* Washington: USCC, 1987. See the section on resources for Southeast Asian Communities, Black Communities, Hispanic Communities, Native American Communities, and Intercultural and Interracial Relations.

Scheduling

1. *The Code of Canon Law,* canons 905 and 1118.
2. Congregation for Divine Worship. *Directory for Sunday Celebrations in the Absence of a Priest.* 1988, nos. 8 and 10.
3. *Province of Chicago Ecumenical Guidelines,* 1986, nos. 105 – 108.

Style

1. Bishops' Committee on the Liturgy. *Concelebration Guidelines,* 1987.
2. Bishops' Committee on the Liturgy. *Liturgical Music Today,* 1982.
3. Bishops' Committee on the Liturgy. *Music in Catholic Worship,* 1972.
4. Bishops' Committee on the Liturgy. *Study Text 5: Eucharistic Concelebration,* 1978.

5. Catholic Conference of Illinois. A *Unique Grace: Statement on Episcopal/Roman Catholic Marriages,* 1990.

6. Paul Covino, ed. *Celebrating Marriage. Preparing the Wedding Liturgy: A Workbook for Engaged Couples.* Washington: Pastoral Press, 1987.

7. Austin Fleming. *Parish Weddings.* Chicago: Liturgy Training Publications, 1987.

8. *Province of Chicago Ecumenical Guidelines,* 1986, nos. 28, 37, 39, 40 – 41, 60 – 62, 101 – 102, 95 – 115, and Appendix on Non-Catholic Ministers Preaching in the Catholic Church.

9. *The Rite of Marriage,* nos. 6 – 11.

§700

THE ORDER OF CHRISTIAN FUNERALS

▪

contents

§700

THE ORDER OF CHRISTIAN FUNERALS

Introduction

The *Order of Christian Funerals* describes the church's ministry to the deceased and their family in these words:

> At the death of a Christian, whose life of faith was begun in the waters of baptism and strengthened at the eucharistic table, the church intercedes on behalf of the deceased because of its confident belief that death is not the end nor does it break the bonds forged in life. The church also ministers to the sorrowing and consoles them in the funeral rites with the comforting word of God and the sacrament of the eucharist. (*Order of Christian Funerals*, #4)

Christians celebrate the funeral rites to offer worship, praise, and thanksgiving to God for the gift of a life which has now been returned to God, the author of life and the hope of the just. The Mass, the memorial of Christ's death and resurrection, is the principal celebration of the Christian funeral.

The celebration of the Christian funeral brings hope and consolation to the living. While proclaiming the Gospel of Jesus Christ and witnessing to Christian hope in the resurrection, the funeral rites also recall to all who take part in them God's mercy and judgment and meet the human need to turn always to God in times of crisis (*Order of Christian Funerals*, #4, 5, 7; *Catechism of the Catholic Church*, #1680–1684).

Ordinarily, Catholics bring the remains of the dead to the church. This is where their Christian journey began. In the waters of baptism they were joined to Christ, who stands victorious over death. This is where they were formed by the Word of God and fed at the Lord's table. The parish church is a symbol of the ecclesial community to which they belong.

The funeral liturgy is not merely a celebration of the bereaved family. It is a celebration of the whole church joined in prayer over the death of one of its members. This is especially important to remember in those times when the members of the bereaved family have not been active members of the church.

Praying for the dead is an expression of communion with them, our love for them, and our desire for their final glory. Comforting those who mourn is a truly Christian response to the unique suffering of those affected by death.

§701

Preparation for Christian Burial

The ministry of consolation is a preeminent part of the ministry of the church. Caring for the dying, praying for the dead and comforting those who mourn are elements of a ministry of consolation. The church calls each member of Christ's Body — priest, deacon, religious, lay person — to this ministry (*Order of Christian Funerals*, #8).

"Each member of the Christian faithful shares in this ministry according to the various gifts and offices in the church" (OCF, #9). The parish community should also recognize that some families have their own circle of family and friends who likewise exercise a ministry of consolation to the bereaved.

The principal means of the community's involvement in the ministry of consolation to those who have suffered the loss of a loved one are often liturgical: the vigil service at the funeral home or in the church, the funeral liturgy and the rite of committal.

Because the funeral liturgies are a crucial part of the church's pastoral care of the grieving, it is essential that they be well prepared and that they include the various roles and ministries that are part of the life of the church.

When the deceased has not been an active Catholic, the presider at the funeral rites needs to make the necessary adaptations in the words that are spoken so as to be sensitive to the reality of the deceased person's life. This can be accomplished especially in the texts which are indicated "in these or similar words," as well as in the homily, the intercessions and the choice of music.

Ministers should avoid any language that might convey a personal judgment of the deceased, remembering the words of eucharistic prayer IV: "whose faith is known to you alone."

At the time of death, families who may not have been active members of the church need to be welcomed in a Christian spirit and helped to feel at home with the church. This can be a fruitful time of evangelization. Through sensitive pastoral care the faith of bereaved family and friends may be rekindled.

Part of the priest's ministry to the grieving family may include the offer to celebrate the sacrament of reconciliation. This is especially appropriate in cases where the family has not attended church for some time. However, conditions do not warrant the offer of general absolution.

The ministry of consolation should extend beyond the liturgy to include the days and weeks following Christian burial. The formation of a bereavement ministry in all the parishes of the archdiocese is strongly encouraged. However, the services that the ministers of bereavement offer should never be perceived as an imposition on the grieving family.

This entire document on Christian funerals should be read in conjunction with the *Order of Christian Funerals*, 1989 edition. All previous editions of the *Order of Christian Funerals* should be retired.

§701.1   Entitlement to Church's Ministry at Time of Death

701.1.1 Policy *Every Catholic, unless specifically excluded according to the norms of law, is entitled to the church's ministry at the time of death.*

Procedures

a) In coordination with the parish priest and the funeral director chosen by the family, the family of the deceased arranges the place and sets the time for the visitation and funeral.

b) The church encourages the celebration of the funeral Mass for one of its deceased members. Sometimes people will hesitate to have a funeral Mass because of doubts about their own faith or worthiness or that of the deceased. In such cases, the judgment of the pastoral minister is essential. It should be explained that the funeral Mass is a prayer for God's mercy for the deceased and solace for the living, and does not presume a life of exemplary faith or virtue.

c) An individual cannot be denied the full rites of Christian burial because of mental retardation or because an infant is multiply handicapped (See Policy 106.5.1, herein).

d) Catechumens are entitled to the full rite of Christian burial. Even though they are unbaptized, they are members of the household of the church (canon 1183.1).

e) In the archdiocese of Chicago, Catholic burial, including the funeral Mass, is permitted for a baptized non-Catholic who might reasonably be presumed to desire or prefer Catholic burial services. Such a decision would be appropriate where the non-Catholic party worshiped regularly at the Catholic church or identified with the Catholic church more than any other. It would not be appropriate if the deceased were an active member of a non-Catholic Christian church, except in cases where the minister of the deceased was unavailable (canon 1183.3).

f) To avoid breaking close family ties, non-Catholic members of Catholic families may be interred in a Catholic cemetery. A Christian burial permit must be issued and presented to the cemetery. Clergy of other communions, vested if they desire, may conduct the cemetery rites according to their own tradition, if the family so desires or if it was the expressed wish of the deceased.

g) The church encourages the burial of Catholics in Catholic cemeteries (canon 1180.1). Parish ministers should attempt to make Catholics aware of the profound reasons for this.

   Burial in a Catholic cemetery is a long-standing sign of the church's reverence for the human body. Appropriately, the ground in Catholic cemeteries is consecrated to receive sacred remains. Burial in a Catholic cemetery recognizes baptismal commitment and gives witness, even in death, to our belief in the resurrection.

   The church maintains Catholic cemeteries because both in life and in death we belong to the Lord (Romans 14:8). Just as the faithful have shared and celebrated their faith in the community of the church, so in death their bodies rest with other deceased members of this community, awaiting the day when God will raise their mortal bodies to glory. Catholic cemeteries stand as a sign to the world that even in death, Catholics believe in life. The images of saints in Catholic cemeteries and mausoleums are not mere decorations; they are a sign of belief in the living communion of saints.

h) A child who dies before baptism may be given Christian funeral rites if the parents intended to have the child baptized (canon 1183.2). The family of the deceased child and the parish priest should determine the appropriate funeral rites for the child (*Catechism of the Catholic Church*, #1261).

i) Burial in a Catholic cemetery is available to every Catholic who, at the time of death, is entitled to receive such burial. Inability to meet the cemetery costs is no deterrent to Christian burial in a Catholic cemetery.

j) When a family is faced with financial hardship, the parish priest or the funeral director should contact the resource consultant at Catholic Charities (312-236-5172). The consultant will describe sources of public and private funds available for assistance and recommend the nature and degree of charitable assistance to be given by the Catholic Cemeteries. Priests whose responsibilities include the spiritual care of patients or residents at various institutions and hospitals may initiate action for charity burials when the deceased has no relative to do this.

k) Effort on the part of parish staffs needs to be made for people with disabilities who live apart from their families in various residential settings so that their bodies are claimed for Christian burial.

l) There is no objection to Catholics making prior arrangements to donate their bodies or parts of them to advance medical science. The only limitation is that, upon eventual disposition of the body or its parts, there be some reasonable assurance that the remains will be disposed of in a proper, reverential manner.

m) The family of the donor should be encouraged to celebrate a memorial Mass as soon as possible after the person's death. Depending upon the circumstances of the donation, the donor's family may choose to have a time for visitation. Whatever remains of the donor's body after an organ transplant or medical research should be given appropriate burial. The rite of committal with final commendation (OCF, #224–233) might appropriately conclude our prayers for the donor and for the donor's family (*Catechism of the Catholic Church*, #2300–2301).

n) With continual respect for the human body, the remains of fetuses or stillborns of Catholic parents and the amputated extremities of Catholic individuals are to be given reverent Christian burial. A Christian burial permit should be issued by the parish priest or deacon, authorized pastoral minister or hospital chaplain. These remains may be placed either in specific individual graves or in a common burial area.

o) The chaplain's office at Catholic hospitals works closely with families in preparing such burials by contacting a funeral director when necessary and the parish of the family involved. When these burials are not handled directly through Catholic hospitals, families should be advised to make arrangements through a local funeral director.

Involvement of Entire Community   §701.2

701.2.1 Policy *Since the ministry of consolation belongs to the entire Christian community, the entire community is to be involved in caring for the dying, praying for the dead, and comforting those who mourn.*

Procedures

a) Catechesis is encouraged to help parishioners understand their role in ministering to those who have suffered the loss of a loved one.

b) Parish policies, procedures, and ministerial resources are to be communicated to parishioners so that they can take full advantage of the services available to them in their time of grief.

c) Parish staffs are to establish clear parish policies and procedures regarding the involvement of lay ministers in the *Order of Christian Funerals.* These parish policies should be established in consultation with the parish liturgy committee and parish pastoral council, and should conform to canon law and the policies and procedures of the archdiocese.

d) Funeral directors provide an invaluable service to families. The family chooses the funeral director based upon professional standards, long service in the community, church participation or friendship.

   Individual funeral directors may perceive and conduct their work for a family as a true pastoral service. Oftentimes the funeral director is the first person in communication with a family who has experienced the death of a loved one. It is important for parish staffs and funeral directors to work together in order to provide the best pastoral care for the bereaved family.

§702

The Ministers and the Rite for the Order of Christian Funerals

When speaking about the presiding minister, the *Order of Christian Funerals*, #15, states:

> Priests, as teachers of faith and ministers of comfort, preside at the funeral rites, especially the Mass; the celebration of the funeral liturgy is especially entrusted to pastors and associate pastors. When no priest is available, deacons, as ministers of the word, of the altar, and of charity, preside at funeral rites. When no priest or deacon is available for the vigil and related rites or the rite of committal, a lay person presides.

§702.1 Implementing the Rite

702.1.1 Policy *In keeping with the norms found in the* Order of Christian Funerals, *priests and deacons are to share the responsibility for planning and implementing the* Order of Christian Funerals *with qualified lay ministers.*

Procedures

If a priest, deacon or parish minister is present when the family first visits the body, the rite Gathering in the Presence of the Body (OCF, #109 – 118) may be used.

702.1.2 Policy *Every effort is to be made to implement the full range of ministries and promote active participation in the liturgies which compose the* Order of Christian Funerals.

Procedures

a) The *Order of Christian Funerals* recommends that the full complement of liturgical ministers (readers, musicians, ushers, pallbearers, communion ministers, servers, etc.) be involved in the conduct of the liturgy (OCF, #15, 33).

b) The parish staff should invite family members to take an active role in the liturgical ministries to the extent to which they are able (OCF, #15, 17). Ministers of consolation should consult the family in the planning and celebration of the funeral liturgy, sharing with them the available options. The preparation of the liturgy can be part of the ministry of consolation. The primary concern is to prepare the family for the liturgy, not just to select the options in the liturgy. The preparation of the liturgy should never become a burden for the family.

c) The *Order of Christian Funerals* recommends that family members be involved in some of the liturgical roles, unless they prefer not to be involved (OCF, #15). For example, the family might be asked to designate the persons who will place the pall or other appropriate symbols upon the casket during the rite of reception of the body at the church as well as the persons who will bring gifts of bread and wine to the altar at Mass (OCF, #152).

d) Music selected for the *Order of Christian Funerals* should be appropriate for Christian prayer and complement the rite being celebrated. The texts of the music should express the paschal mystery of Christ's suffering, death, and resurrection and be related to the Word of God (OCF, #30). Popular non-religious songs should not be used.

§702.2   Presiding at the Vigil

702.2.1 Policy *When priests or deacons are unavailable to preside at the vigil, lay ministers or any fully initiated Catholic who has been properly prepared may appropriately preside. Parishes shall not exclude priests or deacons from presiding at these rites.*

Procedures

a) During the wake, the vigil service is the norm and should not be replaced by other forms of prayer. However, other additional forms of Catholic devotional prayer, such as the rosary, are permitted at another time during the wake.

b) When a wake takes place in the church and the funeral Mass is celebrated that same day or evening, the vigil service is not celebrated. Instead, the prayers for the reception of the body at church are used.

c) Particular parish groups, e.g., the parish senior citizen's club, may be invited to celebrate a prayer service for the deceased in addition to the vigil service.

§702.3   Presiding at the Funeral Liturgy

702.3.1 Policy *When one of its members dies, the church especially encourages the celebration of the Mass (OCF, #46).*

Procedures

a) A parish cantor can be most helpful in leading the congregation in song. A parish funeral choir can also assist at the liturgy.

b) Only an ordained priest or deacon is allowed to preach the homily at the funeral liturgy. Other persons may speak briefly at the wake service or at the beginning of the final commendation. A eulogy is never appropriate where a homily is prescribed (OCF, #27), but examples from the person's life may be used in the homily.

702.3.2 Policy *It is the custom in the United States for a priest or deacon to preside at the funeral liturgy, even if it is celebrated outside of Mass.*

Procedures

The Funeral Liturgy Outside of Mass (OCF, #177–203) is celebrated when a Mass is not possible or not deemed appropriate. It is ordinarily celebrated in the parish church, but it may also be celebrated in a funeral home or cemetery chapel (OCF, #179). The pastoral judgment of the parish priest is essential in determining what is appropriate.

Presiding at the Committal Service   §702.4

702.4.1 Policy *Priests, deacons, trained lay ministers, and any fully initiated Catholics who have been properly prepared are appropriate ministers at committal services when the presider of the funeral Mass is unable to be present at the committal.*

Procedures

a) The rite of committal, the conclusion of the funeral rites, is the final act of caring for the body of the deceased member of the church (OCF, #204). The movement to the cemetery is a ritual procession to the final resting place of the deceased. For the continuity between the Mass and this part of the funeral liturgy, prayers, psalms and songs are recommended for the journey. While this is difficult with an automobile cortege, individuals are encouraged to maintain a spirit of prayer from the church to the cemetery.

b) The wishes of the family should be carefully considered in arranging for the presider at the committal service.

c) As at the funeral Mass, every effort is to be made to assist the assembly in taking a full and active part in the committal by making the appropriate responses and singing the appropriate hymns or acclamations.

d) The committal service may reflect the language and customs of the family of the deceased.

e) While the funeral director's services to the family certainly can be an expression of the larger community's compassion, the distinctive role of the funeral director does not ordinarily include presiding at the committal service. This is to maintain the integral connection between the pastoral care of the parish and the church's liturgical rites, when a priest, deacon or parish lay minister is available.

§702.5   Funeral Liturgies for Children

702.5.1 Policy *The* Order of Christian Funerals *provides a complete funeral liturgy for children which shall be used whenever a child is brought for Christian burial (OCF, #234 – 342).*

Procedures

a) The *Order of Christian Funerals* provides a complete vigil service, funeral Mass with final commendation and rite of committal for the funeral of a child (OCF, #247 – 249, 319 – 336). Various texts for a baptized child or for a child who died before baptism make the rites fully adaptable to a given situation. The eloquent prayers and words of comfort of the rites for children offer special consolation in this extraordinary situation of bewilderment and pain.

b) A complete funeral liturgy outside Mass for children (OCF, #295 – 315) and a rite of final commendation for an infant (OCF, #337 – 342) also are provided for those circumstances when it is appropriate.

§703

Establishing Funeral Liturgy Schedules

The parish community will want to accommodate the needs of a family by providing a flexible parish policy for scheduling the funeral Mass and other rites in the *Order of Christian Funerals*. Local and cultural or ethnic customs may have a bearing on when funeral rites are celebrated as well as how they are celebrated.

In many parishes a large number of funerals will require special consideration and pastoral planning so that the community can sensitively and adequately respond to the needs of a grieving family.

Since it is good for the community to share in the ministry of consolation, the vigil service ought to be celebrated at a time when many of the community are available to participate. The vigil service may be celebrated in the parish church. The time for the vigil service may be published in the obituary.

Although the funeral liturgy will normally be celebrated in the parish church to which the deceased belonged, it is possible to choose any Catholic church for the funeral liturgy, provided the pastor of that church agrees and the pastor of the deceased has been informed (canon 1177). As a rule, the funeral rites of religious or members of societies of apostolic life are celebrated in their own church or oratory (canon 1179). The funeral Mass may also be celebrated in approved chapels of long-term care institutions and in other approved chapels (canon 1225).

§703.1   Restricting the Number of Funeral Celebrations

703.1.1 Policy *Parishes with many funerals may limit the number of funeral Masses or funerals outside of Mass on any given day. A family might not always be able to have a funeral Mass on the day of preference.*

Procedures

a) A policy limiting the number of funeral Masses on one day is to be set in consultation with the parish pastoral council and liturgy committee and is to be published regularly in the parish bulletin.

   Before setting a policy on the limitations of the number of funeral Masses celebrated on one day, a careful review of the daily Mass schedule, the times for funerals and the availability of visiting priests should be made.

b) This policy must be clearly communicated to the parish and the local funeral directors. Family and funeral directors should understand the reasons for the policy and be assured of the parish's commitment to minister to the grieving family.

c) If a funeral cannot be scheduled on a particular day, ordinarily the funeral will be celebrated on the next day.

d) If two or more families desire it, a funeral Mass may be celebrated for more than one deceased person.

e) Funeral Masses may be celebrated at one of the regularly scheduled daily Masses in the parish or in the afternoon or evening. The parish pastoral council and parish liturgy committee are to be consulted in establishing a parish policy.

f) The funeral Mass has first place among the masses for the dead and may be celebrated on any day except solemnities of obligation, on Holy Thursday and the Easter Triduum, and on the Sundays of Advent, Lent and the Easter Season. In the United States, the Holy Days of Obligation are the feasts of Mary, the Mother of God (January 1), Ascension Thursday, the Assumption of Mary (August 15), All Saints (November 1), the Immaculate Conception (December 8), and Christmas (December 25). (See the *General Instruction of the Roman Missal*, #336.)

g) On days when a funeral Mass may not be celebrated, the funeral liturgy outside Mass is celebrated. A memorial Mass may be offered on another day.

Funeral Outside of Mass Followed By a Memorial Mass §703.2

703.2.1 Policy *The family may choose to celebrate the funeral outside of Mass and schedule a memorial Mass at a later date, as is the practice during the Triduum (OCF, #178).*

Procedures

a) The *Order of Christian Funerals* provides an entire ritual to be celebrated outside Mass whereby the community gathers to hear the message of Easter hope proclaimed in the Liturgy of the Word and to commend the deceased to God (OCF, #177).

b) The ritual for a funeral celebrated outside of Mass may be used for various reasons: when the funeral Mass is not permitted; when in some circumstances it is not possible to celebrate the funeral Mass before the committal, for example, if a priest is not present; when for pastoral reasons the funeral liturgy outside Mass is a more suitable form of celebration (OCF, #178).

Style of Christian Funeral Celebrations

While a community has many ways of showing support for the bereaved and respect for the dead, the church's liturgy enables all to move from grief to hope by focusing attention on the mystery of Christ's death and resurrection. These sacred rites shape and form the Christian community and deepen its convictions.

The *Order of Christian Funerals* provides three brief rites that are models of prayer at significant moments: Prayers after Death (OCF, #101–108), Gathering in the Presence of the Body (OCF, #109–118), and the Transfer of the Body to the Church or the Place of Committal (OCF, #119–127).

In the United States, the church ordinarily celebrates the funeral in three principal ritual moments: the vigil (wake), the funeral Mass and the committal. Although each has its particular ritual, the funeral liturgy is a single movement beginning with the viewing of the body and the greeting of the mourners, culminating in the prayers and farewell gestures at the cemetery (*Catechism of the Catholic Church*, #1686).

The entire assembly should be encouraged to participate in word and song in response to the customary prayers. Parish priests are encouraged to instruct parishioners, musicians and parish liturgy committees for full participation.

Special attention should be given to the numerous options that are offered in the *Order of Christian Funerals* to meet the particular circumstances of the deceased.

Principal Ritual Moments §704.1

704.1.1 Policy *In the United States, the principal ritual moments in the* Order of Christian Funerals *are the vigil (wake), the funeral Mass and the committal. Every effort shall be made to implement the services provided for these occasions in the* Order of Christian Funerals.

Procedures

a) It is presumed that the only rite currently used is the *Order of Christian Funerals,* 1989 edition.

b) A Tridentine Rite funeral Mass is not permitted except in those parishes that are approved sites for Sunday celebrations of Tridentine Rite Masses.

c) A pastoral visit to the family by the priest celebrating the funeral Mass is an expected part of the church's ministry of consolation.

d) Ordinarily, there is only one wake service. When a visiting priest or deacon is asked to say a prayer, he can select an appropriate prayer from the *Order of Christian Funerals* or make use of traditional Catholic prayers (i.e., the Lord's Prayer) as may be the custom of the place.

Place for Committal Service §704.2

704.2.1 Policy *The committal service shall be celebrated at the place of burial or interment and not at the church (OCF, #204).*

Procedures

a) The place for the rite of committal, whether in an interment chapel or at graveside, is designed to gather the community for prayer. Most of the Catholic cemetery personnel who prepare such sites are also members of the church community, extending the concern, love, and support of all the faithful.

b) Military services and certain fraternal rites are also permissible at the cemetery. These other services should be arranged in advance with the local parish priest and coordinated in such a way that they do not disrupt or detract from the integrity of the liturgical committal service.

c) An archdiocesan burial permit, signed by a parish priest, deacon or authorized minister, must be presented at the Catholic cemetery for all burials. It should accurately identify the church status of the deceased. Every parish is to keep a book listing those who have died and have been buried from that parish (canon 1182). The burial permit book may be considered the official parish registry of death. (See §902.5, Death Registers.)

§704.3   Cremation

704.3.1 Policy *While the church recommends that the pious custom of burying the bodies of the dead be observed, cremation is permitted as long as it has not been chosen for reasons contrary to church teaching (canon 1176.3; Catechism of the Catholic Church, #2301).*

Procedures

a) If cremation is to take place, ordinarily this occurs after the funeral Mass is celebrated.

b) If cremation has already taken place before the funeral Mass, the funeral Mass is celebrated but the remains are not brought to the church.

c) In the funeral rites contained in the *Order of Christian Funerals*, it is presumed that cremation will not occur immediately after death. The significance of having the body of the deceased present for the funeral Mass is indicated throughout the Mass texts. Therefore, when the family of a deceased person who has requested cremation is making funeral arrangements, the parish priest should recommend that:

    i) following a wake, or a time of visitation, a funeral Mass be celebrated with the body of the deceased present. (According to current liturgical norms, the cremated remains should not be present either for a funeral Mass or a memorial Mass.)

    ii) following the funeral Mass, the body of the deceased may be cremated. (The funeral Mass concludes with the final commendation in church. The funeral director may wish to thank the worshipers for attending and make any other announcements the family has requested. The body of the deceased is then removed to be cremated.)

    iii) at an appropriate time (hours or days later) the family gathers at the cemetery for burial of the cremated remains. The rite of committal takes place at this time with the inclusion of prayers for committal of ashes (OCF, #406.3).

    iv) if a lengthy time has passed since the celebration of the funeral Mass, the rite of committal with final commendation (OCF, #224–233) may be more appropriate.

d) Special circumstances occur, such as health concerns or out-of-state transport, that prompt families to have their loved ones cremated before making funeral arrangements. If cremation has taken place prior to the celebration of the funeral Mass, the parish priest should recommend:

    i) gathering with family and friends for prayer and remembrance of the deceased.

    ii) celebration of a funeral Mass which would conclude with a blessing of the faithful without the final commendation.

    iii) gathering with family and friends for the interment of the cremated remains at the cemetery. (The final commendation and committal are used at the interment.)

e) There may be pastoral reasons for the parish minister and the family to judge that neither a funeral Mass nor a memorial Mass is appropriate. The most important element to be preserved in this situation is that there be some opportunity for prayer. Whether that prayer takes place at church or at the cemetery, we should express our hope and our trust in God with the grieving family.

f) There are two important focuses when speaking of cremation:

    i) even if cremation is chosen for simplicity, the mourners should not be deprived of an opportunity for prayer; and

    ii) cremated remains should be buried or entombed to provide a recognized place for memorialization of the deceased.

§704.4   Christian Burial Inappropriate

704.4.1 Policy *Under certain circumstances Christian burial is inappropriate. Canon 1184 states that unless they have given some signs of repentance before their death, the following are to be deprived of ecclesiastical funeral rites:*

1) *notorious apostates, heretics and schismatics;*
2) *persons who have chosen cremation of their own bodies for reasons opposed to the Christian faith;*
3) *other manifest sinners for whom ecclesiastical funeral rites cannot be granted without public scandal to the faithful.*

Procedures

a)   Before denying Christian funeral rites to anyone or granting funeral rites to someone with a "notorious" reputation, the parish priest is to consult the Office of the Chancellor. The decision of the archbishop or his delegate in these matter is determinative (canon 1184.2).

b)   Two extremes are to be avoided: 1) harshness toward those who have been estranged from the church and 2) scandalous leniency toward notorious criminals. In some cases, Christian funeral rites may be allowed but publication prohibited. If a Mass of Christian Burial is denied, no funeral Mass whatsoever may be offered for the deceased, whether at the funeral home or any other place (canon 1185). A memorial Mass may be scheduled for a later date.

§704.5   Funeral Offering

704.5.1 Policy *The Bishops of the Province of Chicago have established $150.00 as the limit for the suggested offering for funerals, exclusive of expenses (i.e., musician's fees).*

a) It is appropriate for a parish to request an offering to the church at the time of Christian burial. An inability to provide an offering to the parish will not deprive a person of the funeral rites to which that person is entitled (canon 1181). (See §203.3, Offerings for Weddings and Funerals, herein.)

RESOURCES

Preparation

1. Lawrence Boadt, Mary Dombeck and H. Richard Rutherford. *Rites of Death and Dying*. Collegeville: Liturgical Press, 1988.
2. *Liturgy Documentary Series 8: Order of Christian Funerals: General Introduction and Pastoral Notes*. Washington: United States Catholic Conference, 1989. Pub. no. 990–4.
3. Ministry to the Widowed. *Guide to Groups: For the Widowed and Bereaved in the Archdiocese of Chicago*. Chicago: Archdiocese of Chicago, 1992.
4. *Order of Christian Funerals*. Chicago: Liturgy Training Publications, 1989.
5. *Order of Christian Funerals*, study edition. Chicago: Liturgy Training Publications, 1989.
6. Larry A. Platt and Roger G. Branch. *Resources for Ministry in Death and Dying*. Nashville: Broadman Press, 1988.
7. Virginia Sloyan, ed. *A Sourcebook about Christian Death*. Chicago: Liturgy Training Publications, 1990.

Presiders

1. Canadian Conference of Catholic Bishops. *National Bulletin on Liturgy: The Christian Funeral*. Vol. 22, No. 119. Ottawa: Publications Service, 1989.
2. Peter Gilmour. *Now and at the Hour of our Death*. Chicago: Liturgy Training Publications, 1989.
3. Michael Marchal. *Parish Funerals*. Chicago: Liturgy Training Publications, 1987.
4. John Allyn Melloh. *Order of Christian Funerals: A Commentary*. Collegeville: Liturgical Press, 1989.

Scheduling

1. Joseph M. Champlin. *Through Death to Life: Preparing to Celebrate the Funeral Mass*. Notre Dame: Ave Maria Press, 1990.
2. Flor McCarthy. *Funeral Liturgies*. Long Island: Costello Publishing Company, 1987.
3. *Order of Christian Funerals: Vigil Service & Evening Prayer*, leader's edition and people's edition. Collegeville: Liturgical Press, 1989.

Style

1. Joseph M. Champlin. *Through Death to Life: Preparing to Celebrate the Funeral Mass.* Notre Dame: Ave Maria Press, 1990.
2. Peter Gilmour. *Now and at the Hour of our Death.* Chicago: Liturgy Training Publications, 1989.
3. Michael Marchal. *Parish Funerals.* Chicago: Liturgy Training Publications, 1987.
4. John Allyn Melloh. *Order of Christian Funerals: A Commentary.* Collegeville: Liturgical Press, 1989.
5. *Novenario por los difuntos, Novena for the Dead.* Chicago: Liturgy Training Publications, 1992.
6. *Velorio, Wake Service.* Chicago: Liturgy Training Publications, 1992.